AF411691

BRITISH ART
Mead Art Museum Monographs
Volumes 6 & 7   Winter 1985–1986

Edited by Frank Trapp

Mead Art Museum, Amherst College
Amherst, Massachusetts 01002

Cover:
Sir George Hayter (1792–1871)
Family Portrait With Two Children, 1857
Oil on canvas, 24 × 20″
Museum Purchase
1975.73

TABLE OF CONTENTS

The representation of British art at the Mead Art Museum has by now grown to sufficient substance and size to warrant dedication of this issue of the Mead Monographs to certain aspects of its contents. No longer a mere miscellany of unrelated objects, this body of material has by now assumed useful shape, containing as it does, representative samples of the British contribution in various genres, illustrative of the production of that land with which the history and destiny of our own were once so intimately linked.

Indeed, it is difficult to consider the beginnings of artistic enterprise in the United States without reference to still pertinent, transatlantic ties, particularly with Great Britain. And certain major figures such as Benjamin West (1738–1820) or John Singleton Copley (1738–1815) remained life-long British subjects and concluded most of their professional careers in England. Despite their birth in the American colonies and their close identification with the emergence of an artistic heritage unique to our own shores, they were at the same time products of British culture. To some extent, such ambivalences of allegiance would recur from time to time, as with the Philadelphia-born Charles Robert Leslie (1794–1859), who found himself more at home in England than in Pennsylvania, or with the more famous, later expatriate James A. McNeil Whistler (1834–1903). From that point of view, even the career of John Singer Sargent (1856–1925) was closely tied to his British experiences—as were those of Gilbert Stuart (1755–1828), Washington Allston (1779–1843), or Thomas Sully (1783–1872) before him. So much said, however, it is the present purpose not merely to respect those valued associations but to dwell upon the accomplishments particular to Britain, which form part of the larger European, cultural context that inspired them in the beginning.

As is the case with the much larger and catholic range of the collection of American art at Amherst College, the reserves of British art are richest in eighteenth and nineteenth-century examples. That balance is fitting, if to some extent fortuitous, for our holdings are collectively well suited to illuminate those transatlantic ties to which allusion has just been made. At the same time, the high merit and independent interest of British art is respectably served by those works at hand. Among them, the superb offices of British portraitists may be admired in fine works by the brilliant cadre of painters who served admiring patrons of the late eighteenth and early nineteenth centuries. Particularly as many of these portrayals relate to the interests of the Amherst family over a significant period of years, they hold special local interest—a topic which will be treated in the pages to follow.

Both individually and as a group, the British portraits at Mead recall the eminence attained by the leading advocates of that branch of representation who became prominent in the affairs of the Royal Academy, from the time of its founding in 1768. The earliest presiding officers of that distinguished body—Sir Joshua Reynolds, Sir Benjamin West, and Sir Thomas Lawrence—are all handsomely represented in the Mead collection. So, too, are many of their associates, such as Thomas Gainsborough (1727–1788), John Hoppner (1758–1810), Henry Raeburn (1756–1823), and George Romney (1734–1802). The ambitions of the academicians were not, however, reserved for portraiture alone. On the contrary, Reynolds and his colleagues regarded "History Painting" as the highest form of creative address—the depiction of subjects from classical or religious lore or from the recorded course of the human past. Although the destinies of History Painting were generally less favored in Britain than elsewhere and that branch is less richly represented than portraiture in the Mead Collection, our reserves do include several noteworthy examples. Subjects of the kind by West, Washington Allston and William Rimmer illustrate Anglo-American efforts to reach the intellectual and spiritual levels associated with History Painting. And the very recent acquisition of a major effort of the kind by Angelica Kauffmann, *The Return of Telemachus*, has enhanced our capacity to illustrate that particular side of the enterprises encouraged by the Royal Academy, which numbered her as a founding member. One of the essays here included will treat that topic in detail.

This is not to neglect, however, the appeal of other focci within the collection, quite aside from fine examples of the decorative arts, which have been discussed in a prior issue of the Mead Monographs. For example, the British contribution to the development of watercolor painting as an autonomous mode of expression will be reviewed with reference to a selection of works in that medium. And while the museum's resources in Victorian painting remain comparatively small, they do include several exemplary works, the interests of which will also be discussed in the present issue. And not least of all, some notable examples of relevant works in the print collection will also be discussed. Together, it is hoped that these brief essays will provide the reader a sense of the wealth of these resources at the Mead Art Museum.

In the course of preparation it became evident that the present publication should be expanded beyond the scale of previous monographs in the series. It therefore has assumed the nature of a double-issue, so to speak, so that a wider number of relevant topics could be incorporated within a single volume. Our special thanks are extended to the guest authors who have contributed so admirably to its contents: Duncan Robinson, Director of the Yale Center for British Art, Christine Swenson, Curator of Prints and Drawings at the Smith College Art Museum, and Curator-Designate of Prints at the Detroit Institute of Art, and Professor William W. Heath of the English Department at Amherst College. We are grateful for the special expertise they have individually brought to their subjects at hand. The helpfulness of other institutions in providing the necessary permissions for reproducing works in collections elsewhere is warmly recognized: The Chrysler Museum, Norfolk, Virginia, Detroit Institute of Art, Fitzwilliam Museum, Cambridge, Musée du Louvre, Paris, Public Archives, Canada, The Tate Gallery, London, The Toledo Museum of Art, Worcester Art Museum, and Yale Center for British Art.

Funds for this publication were kindly provided by the Associates of Fine Arts at Amherst. Appreciation for support of this series of publications is duly acknowledged.

And as ever, appreciation is to be expressed to the patience of Irene Farrick of the Mead Art Museum staff for her ability to cope with the practical details of translating the preparatory pieces into an integral, published whole. In this task she was capably aided by Lois La Claire, also of the Mead staff. Many photographs were specially prepared for this publication by Frank Ward.

Frank Trapp

BRITISH PORTRAIT PAINTINGS
by Frank Trapp

From October 23 to November 12, 1967, a special exhibition of the Amherst Family Portraits was presented at Mead. The gallery publication prepared for that occasion is now out-of-print, but its contents, prepared by the late Charles H. Morgan and the Curator of the time, Margaret C. Toole, remain of interest today. Extracts from that text[1] will therefore be incorporated where appropriate in the present publication, which is intended to bring that record up to date. Aside from noting further portraits of the family since acquired for the Collection, it includes a significant number of other examples from that flourishing school of painting which now belong to the Amherst College Collection. Taken together, these pictures form a noteworthy body of artistic material, but at their heart remains the exceptional selection of the Amherst Family Portraits, which comprise an unusual or perhaps even a unique biographical holding amongst public collections in the United States.

Contrary to common assumptions, Lord Jeffery Amherst (1717–1797) played no part in the founding of the college which now bears his family's name. That formidable military hero of the "French and Indian War" had long been dead when Amherst College was founded in 1821. Originally a precinct of Hadley, the town from which the College took its name was separately incorporated in 1759. Any connection with the famous general

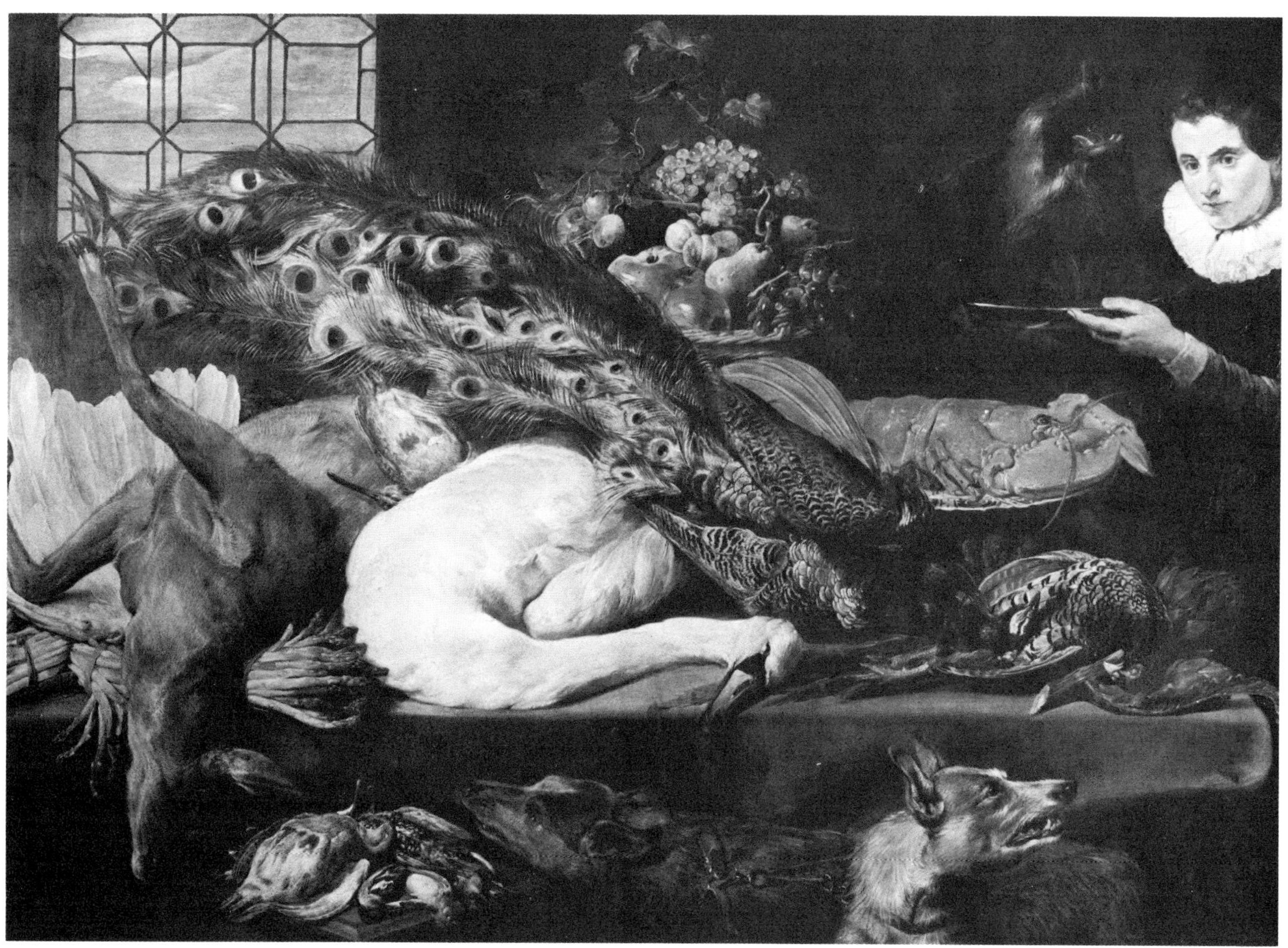

Fig. 1 Frans Snyders (1579–1657)
Still Life
Oil on panel, 55½ × 78½″
Museum Purchase
1962.20

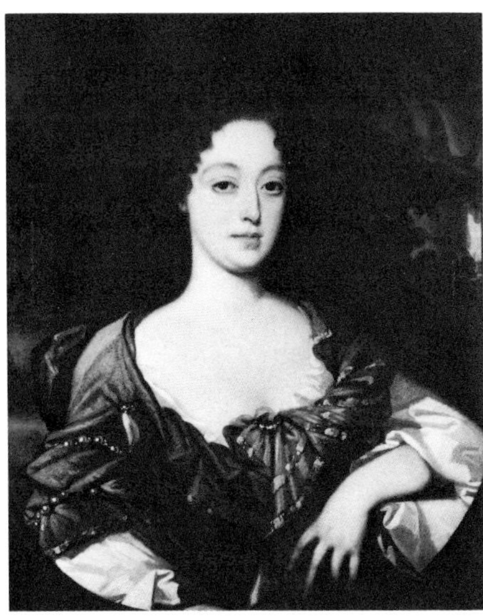

Fig. 2 Sir Peter Lely (1618–1680)
Portrait of Anne, First Wife of Sir Frances Warre
Oil on canvas, 30 × 25"
Bequest of Mrs. Ives Washburn
1964.82

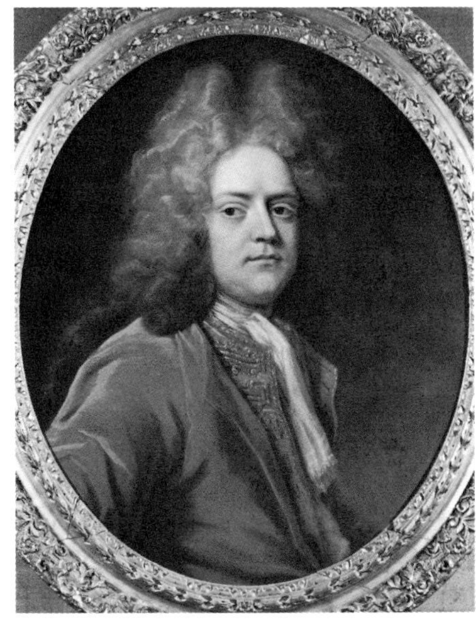

Fig. 3 Sir Godfrey Kneller (1646–1723)
Portrait of James Radcliffe, Earl of Derwentwater
(1689–1716)
Oil on canvas, 30 × 25"
Anonymous Gift
1979.8

was therefore indirect. Admirers of Jeffery Amherst, most notably the long-time President of the Corporation, George Arthur Plimpton '76, were nonetheless eager to foster a more personal association with Lord Amherst, and that image was soon quickened by their enthusiasm. The valuable historical documents amassed by George Plimpton and other members of his family are now preserved in the Archives of Frost Library, Amherst College. And the present Earl, the last member of the Amherst family to succeed to the title, has indeed come to enjoy a friendly relationship with the College—one maintained by his regular visits to the campus over the years. Quite fittingly, the Earl Amherst was honored in 1959, at the time of the bicentennial celebration of the town. Thus, a cherished popular legend had since become a reality.

Thanks to the present Earl's respect and affection for the College, the acquisition in 1967 of a significant group of the Amherst family portraits was facilitated. By then, in 1959, a splendid porcelain dessert service created for the first Earl and his Countess had already found its way to the College Collection. Once confidentially informed of its availability, Prof. Charles H. Morgan had proceeded with dispatch to work out some means of attracting that festive treasure to the College. By another stroke of informed good fortune Morgan found it similarly possible to acquire the splendid painting by Peter Paul Rubens's close associate, Frans Snyders (1579–1657), which had once been part of the Amherst Family Collection (fig. 1). In its new setting it has numerous artistic complements, including other fine Netherlandish paintings of the era; important Flemish Baroque tapestries, one of them based on a similar still-life design by Snyders; and of course, the handsome Rotherwas Room which opens off the main gallery of the Mead Art Museum, in recollec-

tion of the grandness of a former age. (See *Mead Monograph* No. 3)

British desires for portraits had long been served by artists from abroad, most often though not exclusively attracted from the Low Countries. The preeminence of Hans Holbein the Younger (1497–1543) in this capacity at the Tudor Court or later, of Sir Anthony van Dyck (1599–1641) will be remembered. While neither of those major masters is represented in the Amherst College Collection, works by two of their most significant successors on the English scene do appear. Two portraits of women by Sir Peter Lely (1618–1680) exemplify the ease and fluency of portrayal that earned him favor with the patrons of his adopted land (fig. 2). The distinction of another artist from the continent, Sir Geoffrey (Godfrey) Kneller (1646–1723) can be appreciated in a fine portrait of James Radcliffe (fig. 3). And the services of yet another imported artist, Guilliam de Ryck (1635–1699), were enlisted by the immediate forebears of Jeffery, Lord Amherst, in whose features alertness is fashionably combined with dignity and composure (fig. 4).

A school of native British artists and craftsmen did emerge in due course, among them, the portraitist, Thomas Hudson (1701–1779), who is best known as a teacher of the young Joshua Reynolds (1723–1792), who would rise to eminence as a founder and First President of the Royal Academy. One of Hudson's numerous followers was employed by the parents of Jeffery, Lord Amherst, to provide further pieces of the family record (fig. 5). The interest of these portrayals is mainly biographical, however, for they reflect the rigidity of style and execution for which Hudson himself has since been criticized, despite the comfortable reputation he enjoyed in his own day. From that point of view, a recently acquired *Portrait of an Unknown Woman* by George Beare (fl. 1742–49) presents a more attractive sample of an emergent English school, headed above all by William Hogarth (1697–1764). Beare's canvas is discussed in more detail elsewhere in the present publication.

With regard to the personal look of Jeffery, Lord Amherst himself, we are indeed very fortunate in having portraits painted at three different stages of his life, each by an artist of very contrasting stripe. The earliest is a canvas by Joseph Blackburn (1700[?]–1763) painted in 1758, at a time when Amherst was an active military participant (fig. 6). Blackburn had by this time gravitated

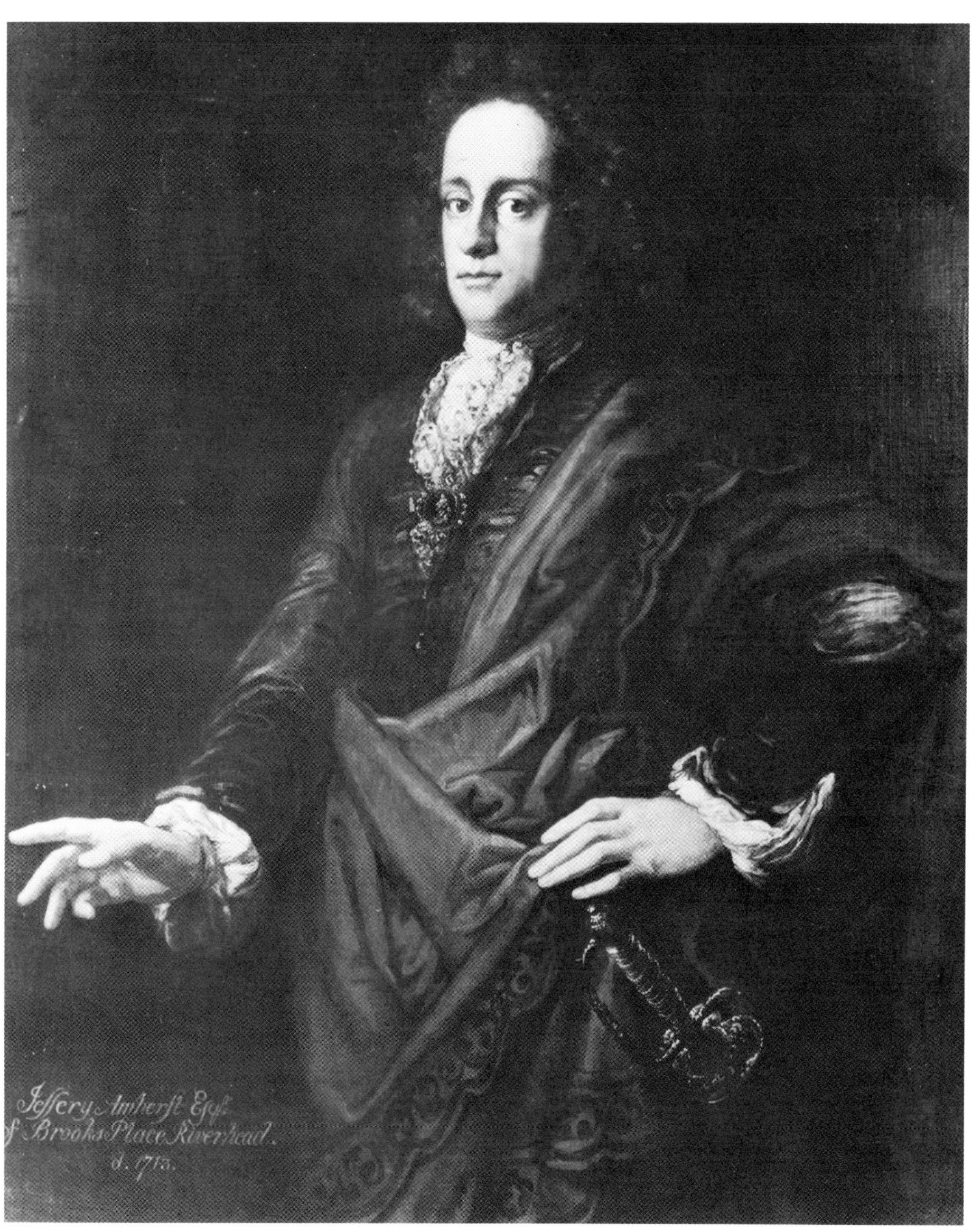

Fig. 4 Guilliam de Ryck (1635–1699)
Portrait of Jeffery Amherst, Esquire
Oil on canvas, 40 × 50″
Gift of Dr. Frank L. Babbott, '13, Francis T. P. Plimpton, '22, Eustace Seligman, '10, Winthrop Smith, '16
1955.326

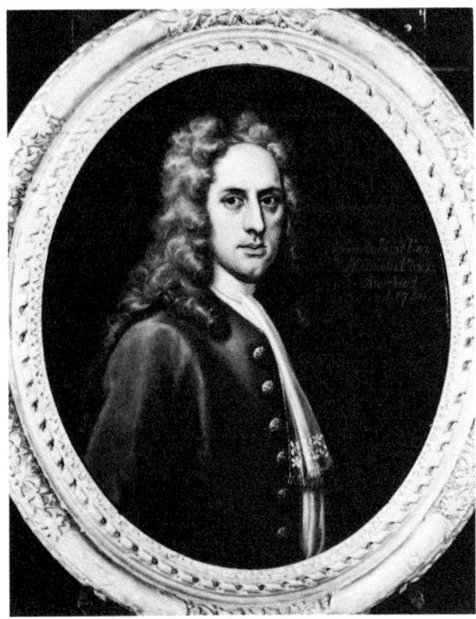

Fig. 5 School of Thomas Hudson (1701–1779)
Portrait of Jeffery Amherst Esquire, 1750
Oil on canvas, 29 × 23¾″
Gift of Charles H. Morgan
1940.2

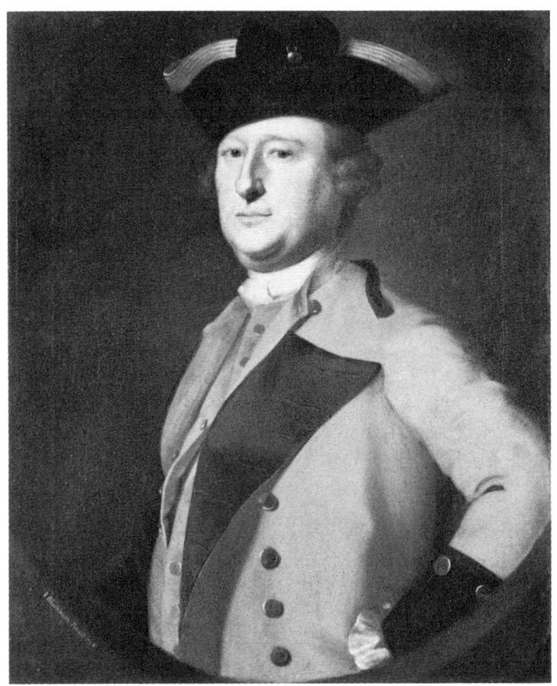

Fig. 6 Joseph Blackburn (1700?–1763)
Sir Jeffery Amherst, 1758
Oil on canvas, 26½ × 32″
Gift of Mrs. Richard K. Webel
1972.1

to the American Colonies, where with his compatriots John Smibert (1688–1751) and Robert Feke (1705 ?– 1750 ?), he plied the same trade. Blackburn's portrayal is of unusual interest for its forthright characterization of a career officer, with a vigorous intelligence and sense of command. Amherst's family background and the circumstances of life which led to his rise to high station and its responsibilities have been summarized in the earlier text prepared by Morgan and Toole. (See Appendices I, II)

The portrait (fig. 7) of General Amherst's brother and fellow officer in His Brittanic Majesty's service, Vice-Admiral John Amherst (1718–1778) was painted by Richard Wilson (1714–1782). Subsequently known primarily as a painter of landscapes, Wilson here shows his mettle as a portraitist. Schooled in the practices of Hudson and his following, Wilson converted their formulas, to achieve results more animated in touch and expression. Depicted at a younger age and probably less demanding circumstances than his slightly older brother faced at the time he sat for Blackburn's portrait, Wilson's young career officer exudes a less intense or energetic sense of personal presence. To some extent, however, that gentler interpretation is consistent with the qualities Wilson cultivated in the landscape subjects, to which he primarily turned from about 1750 onward. Although he had sufficient reputation as a portraitist to rank him among the original members of the Royal Academy, it is almost exclusively for his masterly performance as a founder of a native British landscape school that Wilson is admired today. Still, the professional ease of his early performance as a portrait artist is nicely spoken in this sample of his efforts of a time when he was still ambivalent about his future professional direction.

A later stage of Jeffery Amherst's own career is memorialized in the impressive portrait of him (fig. 8) by Sir Joshua Reynolds (1723–1792). Conceived with the grandiloquence Reynolds found rhetorically appropriate, this image celebrates Amherst's role in the British victory over the French forces at Montreal, which concluded the lengthy struggle between the two colonial

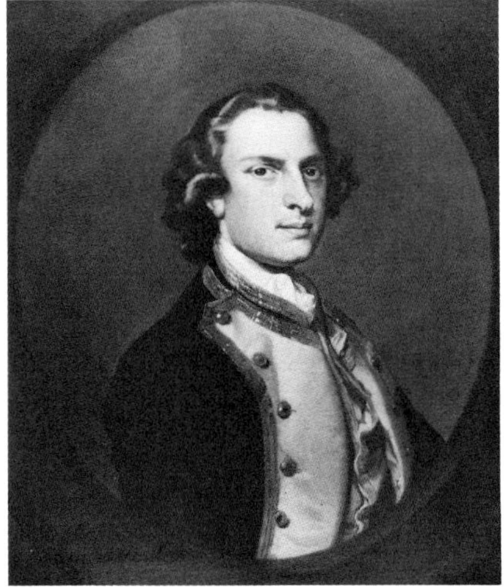

Fig. 7 Richard Wilson (1714–1782)
Portrait of Vice-Admiral John Amherst (1718–1778),
1749
Oil on canvas, 29½ × 24″
Museum Purchase
1967.86

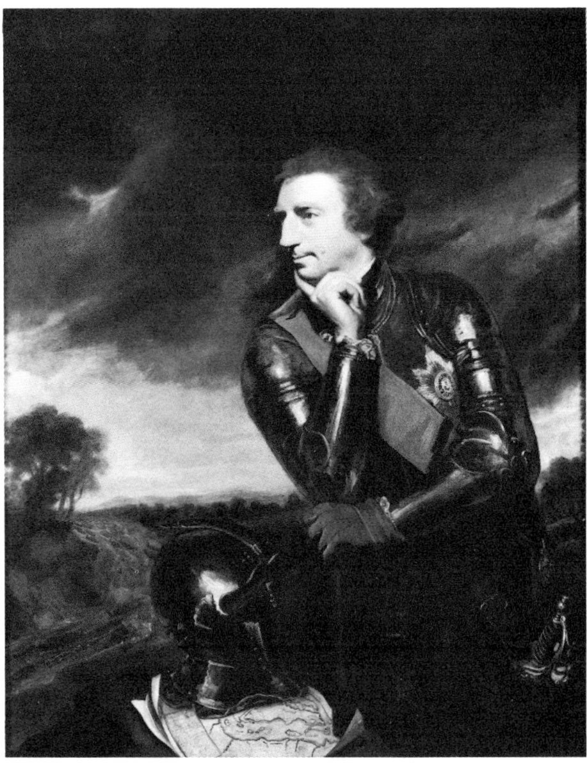

Fig. 8 Sir Joshua Reynolds (1723–1792)
Portrait of Sir Jeffery Amherst, 1765
Oil on canvas, 49 × 34"
Museum Purchase
1967.85

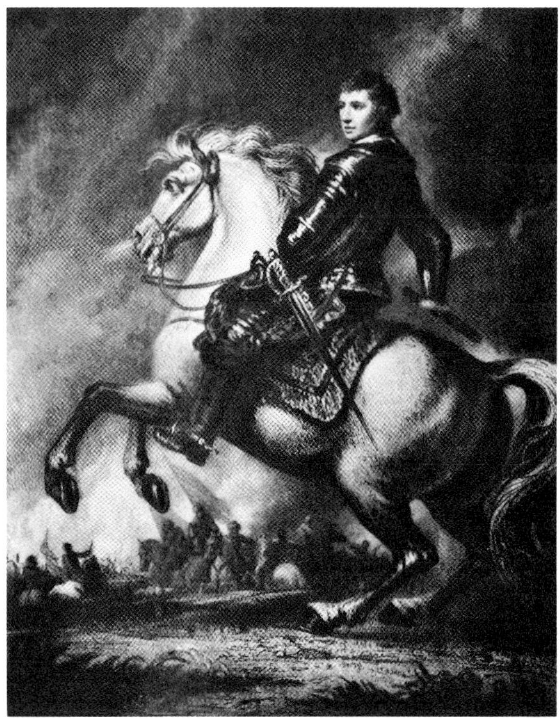

Fig. 9 Samuel William I. Reynolds (1773–1835) after
Sir Joshua Reynolds (1723–1792)
General Amherst. 1822
Mezzotint, 8 × 5¾"
From the James Turner Estate
1946.20

powers for supremacy in North America. Sir Jeffery is shown in ceremonial armour, proudly displaying his well earned decorations as a Knight of the Order of the Bath. The map showing beneath his casque and the landscape beyond both refer to the campaign which culminated in the French defeat.[2]

Comparisons are necessarily drawn between the Amherst College portrait and a replica now to be seen in the National Portrait Gallery, Ottawa, Ontario. Their subject came to be widely known through engraved reproductions. Among them, a mezzotint copy of an equestrian portrait, also by Reynolds, is of exceptional interest. As an example of the engraver's art as practiced in Britain during the late eighteenth and early nineteenth centuries, it deserves admiration in its own right. Another article in the present monograph will treat other graphic works of its kind which are now part of the print collection.

Reynolds' own accomplishments as a painter are also attested in an oil portrait of an as yet unidentified subject, which has upon recent cleaning proved to be an attractive fragment of a larger composition, possibly a double portrait (fig. 10). That supposition is based upon the reappearance of a hand holding a book which survived the cutting of the canvas at what would seem to have been a still unfinished state. The removal of a gummy overlay of paint and varnish also disclosed the

true quality of the actually quite nicely painted woman's head, which is rendered in the pale, rather neutralized tones Reynolds often affected—to some extent in Sir Jeffery's visage, as well. His subject is here shown near an urn of a classical design appropriate to the era. If hardly so significant a product of the artistic authority which won its maker such wide acclaim, this handsome fragment is nevertheless a welcome echo of that grander artistry.

The year 1765, when Reynolds' noble portrait of Sir Jeffery was painted, also saw the death of the general's wife of some twenty-two years, Jane Dalison, his second cousin. Two years later, Miss Elizabeth Carey became his second wife. Her portrait (fig. 11) painted by Francis Cotes (1726–1770) follows closely in the tradition of Reynolds, with whom Cotes was associated as a fellow member of the Royal Academy, which had been founded in 1768. The satisfactions of affluence and graciousness Amherst came to enjoy are also to be appreciated in a third, somewhat later portrayal of him (fig. 12) painted by Thomas Gainsborough (1727–1788), who was Reynolds' greatest rival amongst the thriving school of contemporary British portraitists. A typical if not necessarily an outstanding example of Gainsborough's capacities, it is nonetheless a suave interpretation of the features of a man whose life has been blessed by popular admiration and the prosperity it earned him. Again, he

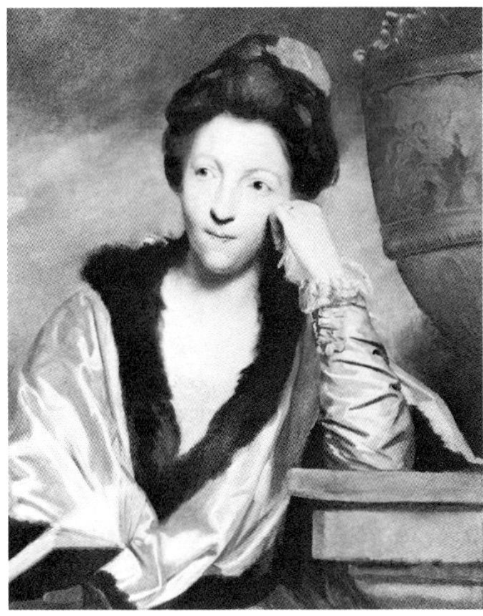

Fig. 10 Sir Joshua Reynolds (1723–1792)
Portrait of Mrs. Barnard, 1767
Oil on canvas, 30 × 25"
Bequest of Herbert L. Pratt, '95
1945.71

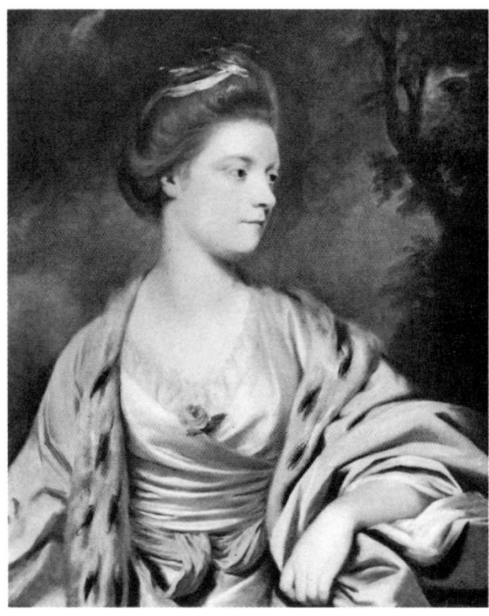

Fig. 11 Francis Cotes (1726–1770)
*Portrait of Elizabeth Carey Amherst, Second Wife
of Jeffery, Lord Amherst*
Oil on canvas, 30 × 25"
Museum Purchase
1967.80

appears in military garb, but now with the powdered coiffeur of an aristocrat of his day, as befitted his newly granted station as Baron Amherst of Holmesdale, later to become Baron of Montreal.

Inasmuch as his second marriage also proved to be childless, Lord Amherst arranged for his titles to be passed on to the son of his younger brother William (1722–1781), who had served as his aide-de-camp during the French and Indian War. The latter (fig. 13), who had also pursued a successful military career, was the subject of a pleasantly informal oil portrait by Robert Edge Pine (c. 1730–1788), a painter of great merit, though never elected a member of the Academy. For whatever reason, Pine eventually moved to Philadelphia where ironically, many of his subjects were veterans of the American Revolution. His career in the new world was brief but flourishing. Pine's penchant for catching his sitter's likeness in a three-quarters view is to be seen here. That trait of composition often served him well in his representations of actors in their theatrical guises—a genre in which he pioneered. Something of that air of fleeting appearance is observable in this portrait of William Amherst. Pine is also represented in the Amherst College Collection by a portrait of William Ash.

While in Pine's case, it may not be appropriate to infer any specific connection of the sort, comparisons may here be noted with the practice of the celebrated Roman painter Pompeo Battoni (1708–1787), who often employed to portray high-born British clients during their lengthy sojourns in Rome, as they experienced the cultural attractions of Italy while on the Grand Tour. A *Portrait of an English Gentleman and his Dog* (fig. 14) closely and very nicely reflects the character of Battoni's

approach, if not perhaps at quite the level of quality normally expected of the master himself. In it a similar air of easy, rather conversational informality may be appreciated. Traits of the sort were, of course, cultivated by British painters of so-called "conversation pieces," group portraits given the informal look of genre pieces. Unfortunately, the Amherst College Collection cannot

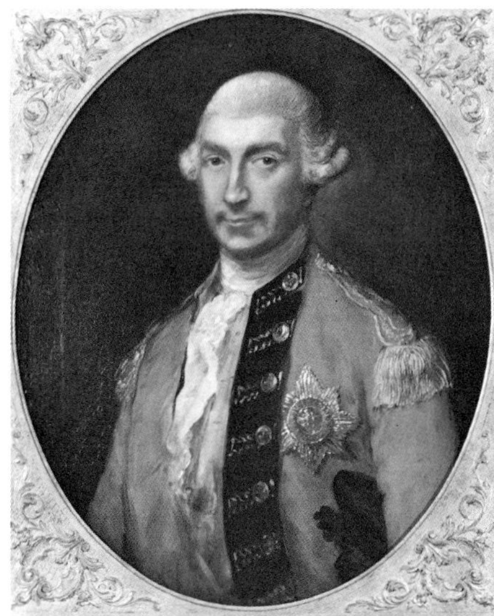

Fig. 12 Thomas Gainsborough (1727–1788)
Portrait of Lord Jeffery Amherst (1717–1797), ca. 1785
Oil on canvas, 30 × 25"
Gift of Mrs. George D. Pratt
P1940.5

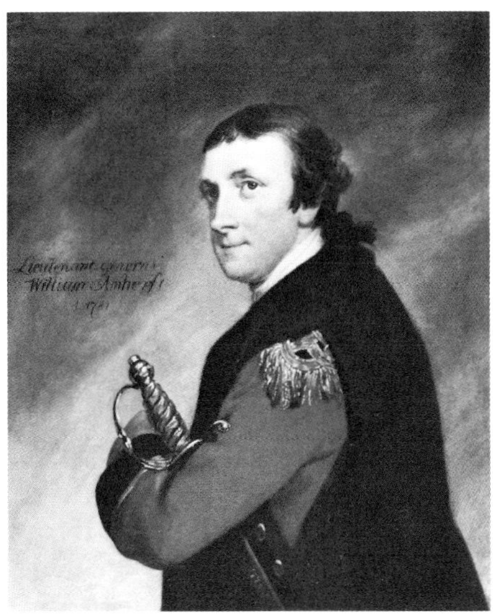

Fig. 13 Robert Edge Pine (1742–1790)
Lieutenant General William Amherst (1722–1781), 1779
Oil on canvas, 30 × 25″
Museum Purchase
1967.83

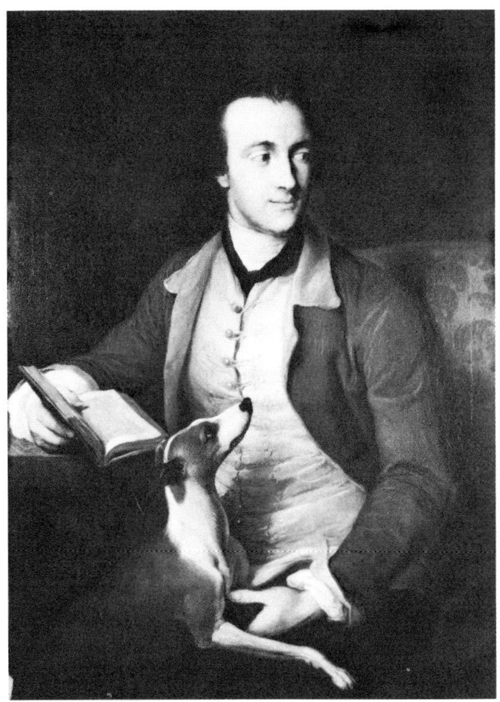

Fig. 14 Circle of Pompeo Battoni (1702/8-1787)
A Man With a Dog
Oil on canvas, 38½ × 28½″
Gift of Miss Hope Gray
1972.17

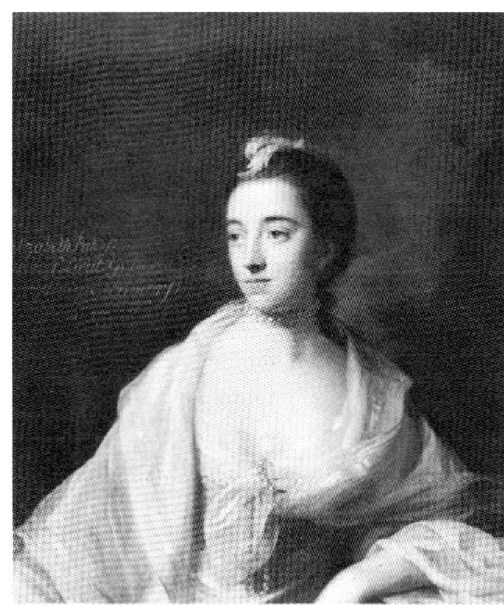

Fig. 15 Allan Ramsay (1713–1784)
Portrait of Elizabeth Patterson Amherst
Oil on canvas, 29 × 24″
Museum Purchase
1967.84

yet boast an example of this latter aspect of the British pictorial heritage, but it may be hoped that this lack will some day be corrected.

Within the more direct, formal tradition of portraiture, however, a portrait of Elizabeth Patterson Amherst, William's wife (fig. 15), affords us a charming example of the art of the Scottish-born Allan Ramsay (1713–1784), in whose works an elegant ease derived of Italian inspiration was lent special grace. His personal variations of the sort, based upon the successful formulas encouraged by Reynolds, illustrate the admirable level of proficiency maintained within the ranks of the leading portraitists of the era.

And while the College Collection does not yet contain any portraiture by George Romney (1734–1802), whose fashionable reputation approached that of Reynolds and Gainsborough, it does include several canvases by the American-born Gilbert Stuart (1755–1828), who shared something of Romney's breadth and ease of execution. Two of these works, *Lady Frances Erskine* and *Robert Shaw of Teremure*, date from Stuart's period spent in England and Ireland, when some of his finest works were done, before the temptations to repetitiousness and superficiality which often creep into his popular production of later years, following his return to his native shores. Amherst College can also boast two fine portraits by Romney's great rival John Hoppner (1758–1810). One of them represents William, *1st Earl of Harewood*. The other (fig. 16), which is marked by like qualities of felicitous touch and attractive characterization, portrays Lord Jeffery's distinguished nephew, the son of William and Elizabeth Patterson Amherst, William Pitt Amherst (1773–1857). Eventually elevated in rank to become the 1st Earl Amherst of Arakan, Lord Jeffery's nephew enjoyed distinctions as a servant of the Crown which rivalled his uncle's accomplishments. (See Appendix III)

Although Hoppner's efforts have sometimes been criticized as overly facile, it would be hard to describe the Pitt portrait in such terms. Exceptionally attractive both in its sense of the presence of its sitter and in its skillful economy and freshness of execution, Hoppner's portrait is one of the most appealing likenesses of the entire family group. Quite fittingly, the Earl's wife, Lady Sarah Hickman Amherst (1762–1837) was painted by the reigning portraitist of the succeeding artistic generation, Sir Thomas Lawrence (1769–1830). If not one of Lawrence's most lavish or important performances, this image of the comely and accomplished 1st Countess Amherst (fig. 17) is a fair reminder of its maker's great flair and serves as a fitting companion to Hoppner's urbane portrayal of her husband. As the Morgan-Toole account observes (p. 17): "The Countess of Amherst in-

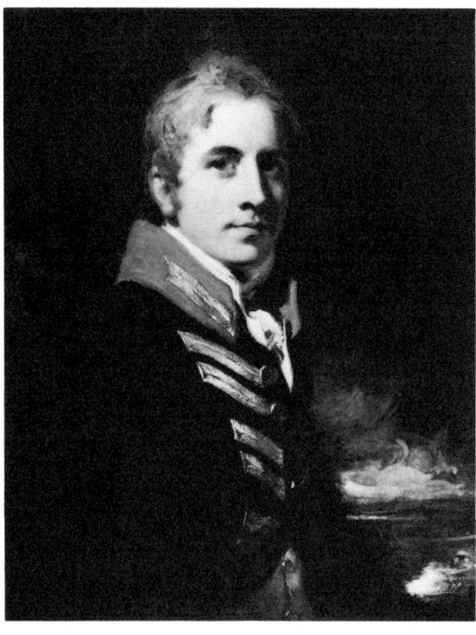

Fig. 16 John Hoppner (1758–1810)
Portrait of William Pitt Amherst (1773–1857)
Oil on canvas, 30 × 25"
Museum Purchase
1967.81

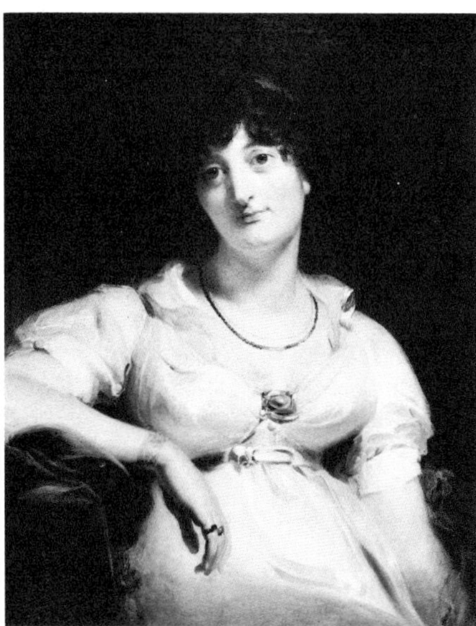

Fig. 17 Sir Thomas Lawrence (1769–1830)
Portrait of Sarah Hickman Amherst
Oil on canvas, 30 × 25"
Museum Purchase
1967.82

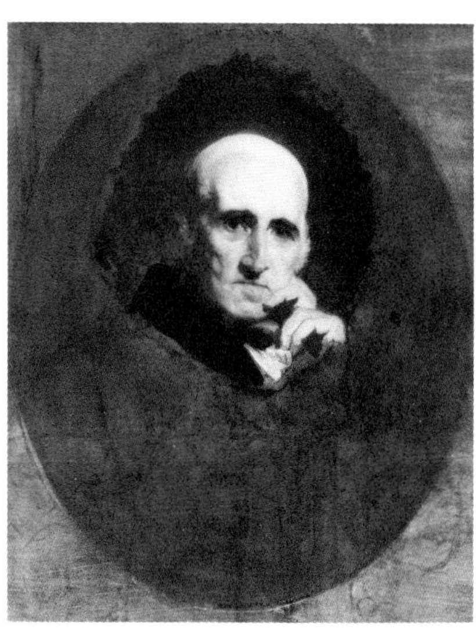

Fig. 18 Sir Thomas Lawrence (1769–1830)
Portrait of Benjamin West (Sketch), ca. 1820–21
Oil on panel, 28⅞ × 23⅞"
Bequest of Herbert L. Pratt, '95
1945.85

spired her own memorials. Great flowering trees, fishing flies, pheasants and china ware still bear her name." A biographical sketch of the capable and enterprising Lady Amherst will be included in a book about notable naturalists now being prepared by Mrs. B. Mearns of Dumfries, Scotland.

By happy chance, the College Collection is also blessed with two other fine portraits by Lawrence, both oil sketches which eloquently testify to his surety and dash. The first of these (fig. 18) represents his teacher, friend, and predecessor as President of the Royal Academy, Benjamin West (1738–1820). Though born in Philadelphia, that fine teacher and diplomat in the world of art was, after Reynolds, a dominant figure in the London scene, one who succeeded Reynolds as President of the Royal Academy. This study for the head incorporated in a large portrait of that master now in the National Portrait Gallery, London, captures the intelligence, seriousness of purpose and generosity that distinguished West's own career. The College is also fortunate in having works by West himself as part of the Mead collection. Among them, a portrait of *Dr. Enoch Edwards*, 1795, is of particular importance in the present context. West's situation within the British scene will, however, be discussed more fully elsewhere in the present publication.

The second Thomas Lawrence study represents Charles Baring Wall (fig. 19). In it are encapsulated all the painter's gifts of freshness and spontaneity, in which the painterly traditions of the Baroque era are reinvigorated. Here they are especially suitable in his capturing the youthful appeal of his sitter's countenance. That responsiveness to the presence of young subjects was an ingratiating capacity cultivated by a number of late eighteenth-century portraitists, especially in Britain and France. Reynolds' own *Age of Innocence* or *Lady Catherine Howard* will be remembered, among others, as charming examples of the taste for the charms of childhood, as well as a new fascination for femininity which then assumed prominence. Lawrence's image of Wall is thus part of a larger turn of mind, as childhood was at the time gaining recognition as something other than a diminutive form of adulthood. Eventually, if only gradually, that awareness of the young in years would be extended to the youthful subjects of lesser station as well, as may be seen in the repertory of nineteeth-century artists, wherein the traditions of Baroque genre painting were tirelessly reinterpreted.

Other worthy exemplars of the British portrait tradition may also be noted at this juncture. The high level of quality maintained by the Scottish artist Henry Raeburn is evident in his animated, forthright image of *Lt. General William Stuart* (fig. 20). The capable George Henry Harlow (1787–1819) is represented by an attractive *Portrait of Margaret Gidding* (fig. 21), and the finesse and dignity sometimes attained in Victorian portraiture are nicely summarized in a sensitive representation of Lady Arnold (fig. 22) by the Scottish artist, James Archer (1824–1904). Nor has the last word been said about the gallery of Amherst family likenesses. In 1982, an impressive, formal portrait of the 4th Earl Amherst (fig. 23),

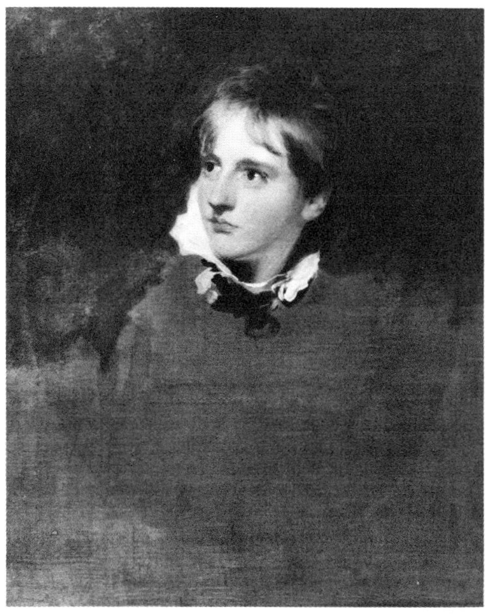

Fig. 19 Sir Thomas Lawrence (1769–1830)
Charles Baring Wall
Oil on canvas, 32 × 27″
Gift of Dwight W. Morrow, Jr., '33
1956.9

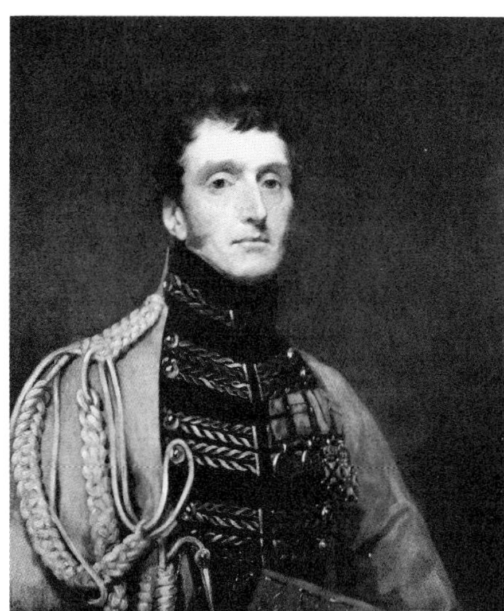

Fig. 20 Sir Henry Raeburn (1756–1823)
Portrait of Lt. General, The Honorable William Stuart (1772–1827), bet. 1815–1823
Oil on canvas, 30 × 25″
Bequest of Herbert L. Pratt, '95
1945.15

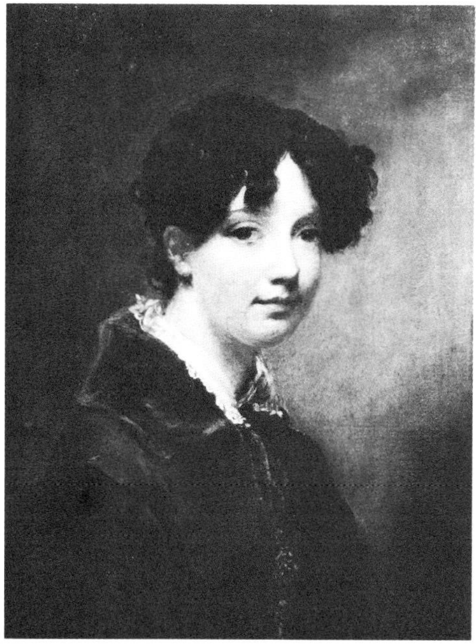

Fig. 21 George Henry Harlow (1787–1819)
Portrait of Margaret Gidding
Oil on canvas, 10 × 8″
Gift of the Estate of Chester Dale
1963.152

painted in 1926 by Alfred Egerton Cooper (1883–1974)
was given to the Collection, to join a stylish likeness of
his son, the present Earl, commissioned of Patrick Procktor (b. 1936) by mutual friends of Lord Jeffery and the
College (fig. 24).

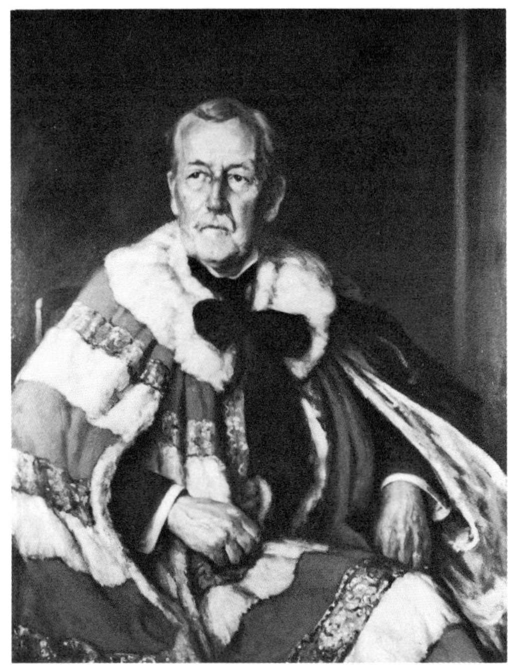

Fig. 23 Alfred Egerton Cooper (1883–1974)
   Portrait of the Fourth Earl Amherst, 1926
   Oil on canvas, 36 × 28¼"
   Gift of the Fifth Earl Amherst, the Rt. Honorable
   Lord Jeffery Amherst
   1982.129

The span of this fascinating succession of person-
alities was thereby extended to include members of the
later generations who have proudly borne the name.
And in the process, the holdings of the Mead Art Museum were further enriched in their capacity to present a
tradition of portraiture which was long maintained with
great distinction in Britain and which had deep significance for the development of the art of portraiture in our
own land.

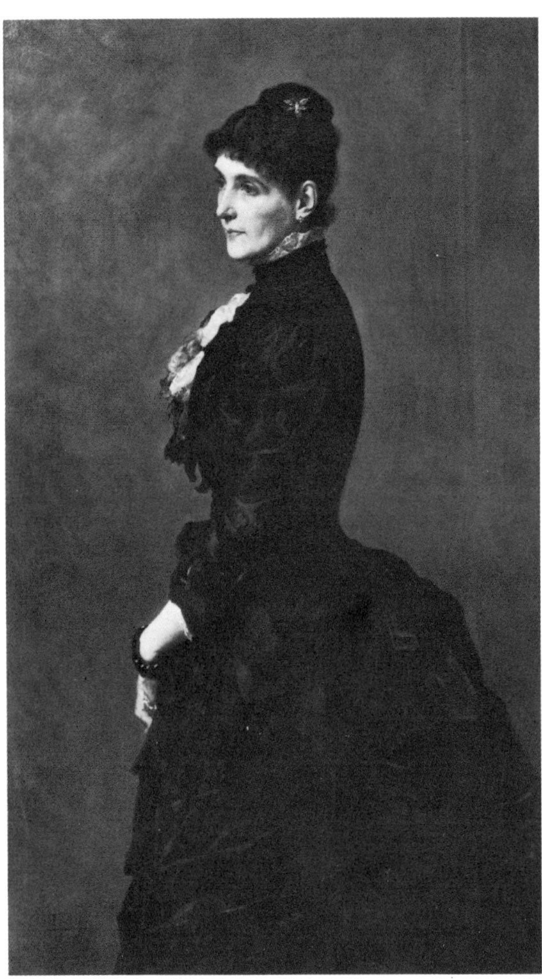

Fig. 22 James Archer (1824–1904)
   Portrait of Lady Arnold, 1885
   Oil on canvas, 53½ × 31½"
   Gift of Laurence Channing in Memory of Fairfield
   Porter
   1980.95

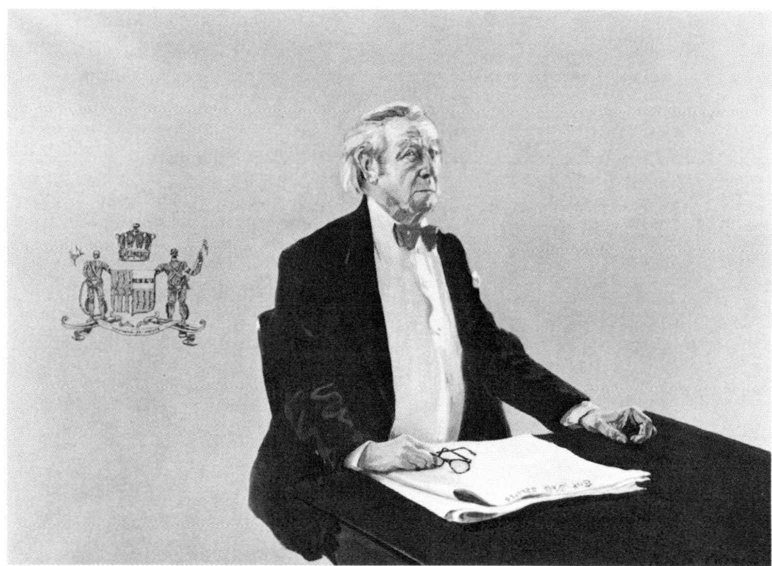

Fig. 24 Patrick Procktor (b. 1936)
Portrait of Jeffery John Archer, 5th Earl
Amherst, 1980
Acrylic on canvas, 28 × 38″
Gift of Charles H. Morgan, Dr. Jack W. C. Hagstrom,
and Mr. and Mrs. T. Dixson Long
1980.96

FOOTNOTES

1. To facilitate reading the present resume, the longer extracts from the earlier text will be included as biographical appendices.

2. Here the landscape reflects the terrain described by one of Amherst's officers, Thomas Davies, in a drawing now preserved in the Public Archives of Canada. Active in the Lake Champlain Campaign during the French and Indian Wars, in 1759, Davies had sketched Crown Point as Amherst rebuilt it. The following year he made this particular drawing (fig. a) which shows the "Passage of Amherst's Army down the Rapids of the St. Lawrence toward Montreal." It bears the painter's own collector's stamp (Lugt 2364) in the lower right corner, so the direct association of the drawing and the completed portrait by Reynolds is nicely documented. Officers of the day were often trained to record the lay of the land for tactical purposes. It is interesting to observe that Reynolds has taken advantage of this kind of specific military observation. See *Archives of Canada Microfiches,* Microfiche 10, 1977. No. B1. See also, *Image of Canada* (Ottawa: Public Archives of Canada, 1972), Nos. 32, 33.

APPENDIX I

The Family Background

Kent is a pleasant shire south and east of London where stand the great country seats of Cobham Hall, Penshurst, Hever Castle and Knole, the home of the Sackville family whose head, during the first half of the eighteenth century, was the first Duke of Dorset, thrice lord Steward of the royal household and twice lord-lieutenant of Ireland.

Within sight of Knole Mr. Jeffery Amherst, barrister and Member of Parliament, lived in a comfortable small mansion called Brook's Place in the village of Riverhead. Here his son Jeffery brought his bride, Elizabeth Kerrill, and began to raise a numerous brood.

Five of these children survived, four sons and a daughter. The friendship between the Amherst family and its powerful neighbors at Knole is affirmed by the choice of the name Sackville for the oldest son. Elizabeth, the only daughter, married Reverend John Hardy and later developed some fame for her poetry. Three younger sons, because of the custom of primogeniture, had their choice of remaining dependents of the family or of making their own way in life. These three sons of Jeffery and Elizabeth Amherst—Jeffery, John and William—chose to carve out for themselves their own careers in the armed services of the crown.

In the eighteenth century a younger son needed four aids to success: money, patronage, ability and luck. The Amherst family was only modestly "well-to-do"; but the Sackvilles had influence. The sons supplied the ability;—and luck was with them.

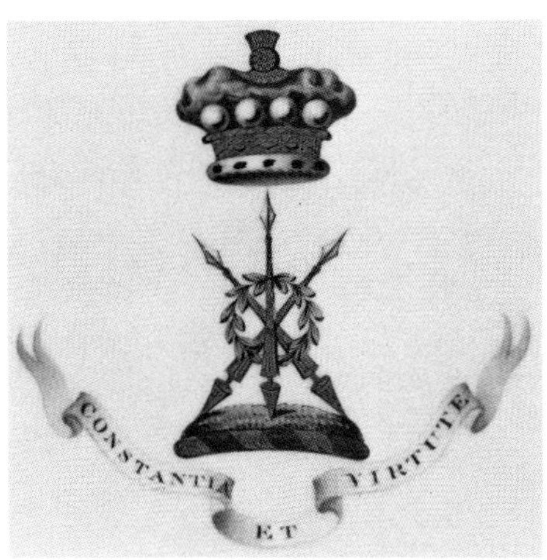

*Jeffery
?–1733
m

1st Elizabeth
Tate

2nd Dorothy
Amherst

*Jeffery
?–1750
m
*Elizabeth Kerrill

Sackville
?–1764

***JEFFERY
1st Baron
1717–1797
m

*John
1718–1778

*William
1722–1781
m
Elizabeth Patterson

Elizabeth

1st Jane
Dalison

*2nd Elizabeth
Carey

Elizabeth

*WILLIAM PITT
1st Earl
1773–1857
m

*1st Sarah
Hickman

2nd Mary
Archer

Jeffery

WILLIAM PITT
2nd Earl
1805–1886
m
Gertrude Perry

Frederick

Sarah

WILLIAM ARCHER
3rd Earl
1836–1910
m

Frederick

Percy

Jeffery

Josceline

*HUGH
4th Earl
1856–1927
m
Hon. Eleanor St. Aubyn

1st Lady Julia
Cornwallis

2nd Alice
Dalton

*JEFFERY JOHN
ARCHER
5th Earl

Humphrey William

Joan

Mary

*Indicates a portrait in the College's collection

APPENDIX II

Colonel Jeffery Amherst:
Prelude on the Continent

Born in 1717 at Brook's Place, Jeffery, the future Lord Amherst, was first employed as a page in the household of the Duke of Dorset where he early became acquainted with a host of "important personages," with their habits, their tastes, and their peculiar talents. The Duke's establishment might be likened to a generous, if unorthodox, preparatory school.

It was the Duke who saw to it that long, lean Jeffery Amherst received an appointment as Ensign in the First Regiment of the Foot Guards when he was eighteen. The Foot Guards attended the king in times of peace, and assumed the most perilous assignments in times of war.

For seven years Ensign Amherst trudged through his daily duties, clad in an incredibly awkward uniform, at the palaces in London and Windsor. In 1742, the War of the Austrian Succession took him to the Continent as aide-de-camp to the brilliant General Ligonier, a veteran of the Battle of Blenheim. In the first year of this campaign Lord George Sackville wrote to the Duke of Dorset: "You cannot imagine how well everybody speaks of Jeff. Amherst." In the Battle of Dettingen he distinguished himself with a fellow officer, one James Wolfe.

The Duke of Cumberland, son of George II, took over General Ligonier's command. By 1747, aged thirty, the one-time Ensign had become a Lieutenant Colonel and aide-de-camp to the duke; and during the years of peace that followed he served as Groom of the Duke's Bedchamber.

In 1750, his father died and his brother Sackville succeeded to the Brook's Place property.

In 1753, Jeffery married his second cousin, Jane Dalison.

A series of "incidents" along the Franco-British frontiers in the New World determined Prime Minister William Pitt, known as the "Great Commoner," to destroy French power in America. General Sir Jean Ligonier was his War Master; and they jointly chose Jeffery Amherst to command a force of eleven thousand men, with the rank of temporary Major General, and charged him with the reduction of the fortress of Louisburg.

General Jeffery Amherst:

Louisburg   Champlain   Quebec

On May 28, 1758, General Amherst's ship sighted off Halifax the forest of sails transporting the men and the guns with which he would take Louisburg. This was the first of the fortuitous timings that would mark his career. The rock-ribbed harbor of Louisburg offered the most formidable defences in North America. Whoever held it controlled the approaches to the St. Lawrence River and New France. The siege was prolonged, for Amherst was never profligate with his troops; but the boldness of

Wolfe and the sagacity of Admiral Boscawen forced the citadel to surrender on July 27th. The General dispatched his aide-de-camp and brother, Captain William Amherst, with the good news to London, arranged for the security of the Gulf of the St. Lawrence, and then departed aboard the ship commanded by another brother, Captain John Amherst, for the port of Boston where a joyful population nearly disrupted the discipline of his command.

During the siege of Louisburg, the French had inflicted a severe defeat on the British at Lake Champlain. The campaign of 1759 consequently centered on securing the New York frontier and the capture of Quebec. These targets were so divided by wilderness and sea that Wolfe was given independent charge of the operation against Quebec. Amherst recaptured Fort Ticonderoga, occupied Crown Point, reduced the French ships on Champlain, and secured his positions in the west. A separate expedition under his command took Fort Niagara. For these services, and at Pitt's insistence, he was made a permanent Major General and given the governorship of Virginia which he held, perforce, *in absentia*.

Late in the summer, Wolfe completed the schedule for the year with his brilliant surprise of the Quebec garrison. The battle on the Plains of Abraham was brisk and brief concluding with the deaths of both Wolfe and his adversary, Montcalm, on the battlefield at the moment of victory.

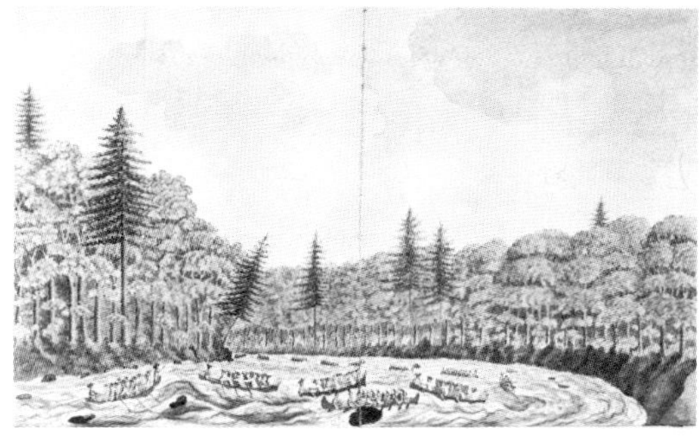

Fig. a Thomas Davies (ca./vers 1737–1812)
Passage of Amherst's Army down the Rapids of St. Lawrence towards Montreal, 1760
Pen and ink and gray wash, 10½ × 16¼"
Photo courtesy of Public Archives, Canada
(Archives publiques, Canada)

Sir Jeffery Amherst:

Montreal   The West Indies   Pontiac's War

One stronghold remained for Amherst to reduce— Montreal. From his headquarters in New York and then in Albany, General Amherst planned a triple thrust. One arm would proceed up the St. Lawrence from Quebec. The second would attack after breaching the last French defenses at the north end of Champlain. He, personally, would command the third and longest, marching across

New York to Lake Ontario and thence eastward by boat down the St. Lawrence. Miraculously the three expeditions converged on Montreal within twenty-four hours, and the town's commander had no choice but immediate surrender. The fall of New France was complete.

The news was greeted on both sides of the Atlantic with a delirium equal to that at the ending of both World Wars. Eight towns in the colonies were named for Amherst, the idol of the hour, who promptly settled down to the reorganization of the conquered territories so successfully that he was called ". . . the greatest administrator produced by England since the death of Marlborough..." Meanwhile, as commander-in-chief in America, he sent off expeditions against the French colony in Haiti and the Spanish port of Havana, and dispatched his brother, Colonel William Amherst, to rout a quixotic landing of the French in Newfoundland. His grateful king, now George III, rewarded him with the gold collar and red ribbon of the Order of the Bath, the first time the investiture of Knighthood had been performed in America. In 1763, Pontiac raised the western Indians in a ferocious attack on the English outposts. Not until this dangerous eruption was brought to a firm conclusion did Sir Jeffery set sail for England after nearly six years in the New World.

With him he took the devotion of the colonials, and the shrubs and seeds he would plant into an American garden in the family seat, Brook's Place, Riverside, Kent.

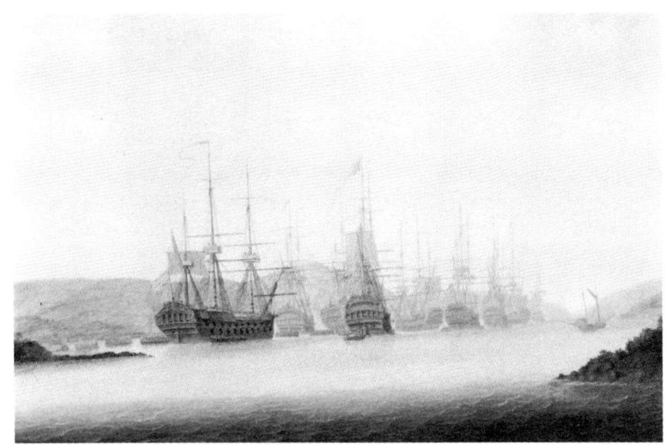

Fig. b William Elliot (?–1792)
Quebec Harbour, 1759
Oil on canvas, 24 × 36"
Departmental transfer
1981.108

APPENDIX III

William Pitt Amherst: 2nd Baron Amherst of Montreal

Lieutenant General William Amherst settled down on the Isle of Wight. He declined to serve against the American colonies, but held a seat in the House of Commons. In 1766, he married "a very pretty and accom-

plished woman," Miss Elizabeth Patterson. Their son was born in the fashionable spa of Bath in 1773 and was named William Pitt for one of his godfathers. Mrs. Amherst died in 1776, the General in 1781; and William Pitt Amherst and his sister moved at once to "Montreal" to be reared as Lord Amherst's own children.

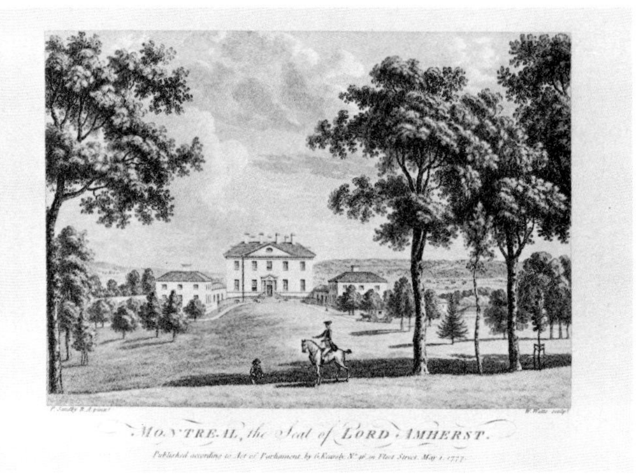

Fig. c William Watts (1752–1851) after Paul Sandby
Montreal, the seat of Lord Amherst, 1777
Engraving, 6½ × 8¼"
Museum Purchase with Funds for the Collins Print Room
1985.29

His uncle sent the boy to Westminster, then on to Oxford. Leaving there in 1793, the future Earl started on the Grand Tour of the continent as befitted a Baron's heir. In the course of his travels he acquired some excellent works of art and a taste for languages that would add to his qualifications for a diplomatic career.

In 1797, he received his Master of Arts degree from Oxford; and that summer Jeffery, Lord Amherst died leaving him his entire estate and the title of Baron he had so hardly earned.

During his stay in Rome, William Pitt Amherst had enjoyed the company of the fifth Earl and Countess of Plymouth. A few years later the Earl died, and in 1800 his widow became Lady Amherst.

From 1802 to 1804, the second Baron Amherst was Lord of the Bedchamber to George III. In 1809, he went to Sicily as Ambassador Extraordinary, and in 1815 he was made a Privy Councillor. The next year the Prince Regent sent him on an abortive mission to China where for the first time he confronted the labyrinthine affairs of the East India Company. He was also shipwrecked; but on his return journey he enjoyed a memorable visit with Napoleon on the Island of St. Helena.

William Pitt Amherst: First Earl Amherst of Arakan

On the death of George III the Prince Regent ascended the throne as George IV. Three years later, he appointed Lord Amherst Governor-General of India and the latter, accompanied by Lady Amherst, set sail to cope with the tangle of recently conquered territories, nebulous boundaries and the East India Company.

William Pitt Amherst, a diplomat at heart and pacific by nature, found himself confronted with a maze of unprecedented colonial problems. Almost at once he found himself engaged in the Burmese War.

For his services in India and Burma, George IV created him Earl Amherst of Arakan and Viscount Holmesdale.

The Countess of Amherst inspired her own memorials. Great flowering trees, fishing flies, pheasants and china ware still bear her name.

Returning to England in 1828, Earl Amherst resumed his customary duties as Lord of the Bedchamber to George IV and William IV. The latter monarch bestowed on him the Knight Grand Cross of the Hanoverian Order. His appointment as Governor-General to Canada was entirely appropriate; but it was annulled by a change in government. The Countess dying in 1837, he married the widow of the sixth Earl of Plymouth, co-heiress of the Sackville home at Knole. There he died in 1857 within sight of "Montreal."

Editor's Note: After the present publication had gone to press a major exhibition of works by Sir Joshua Reynolds opened at the Royal Academy of Arts, London, on January 16, 1986. The catalogue for the exhibition, edited by Nicholas Penny with additional contributions by other scholars (London: Royal Academy of Arts, 1986) constitutes a major source of information on the artist's career. Extensive though it is, however, the catalogue does not — for whatever reason — treat Sir Joshua's representations of Jeffery Amherst. The present commentary thus constitutes in its way a modest addendum to that ambitious presentation of the master's oeuvre.

GEORGE BEARE: A NEW MASTERPIECE
by Duncan Robinson

Thanks to the Amherst Collection, the Mead Art Museum can boast a succession of British portraits which combine genealogical interest with art historical importance. The Amhersts were both prominent enough and sufficiently discerning as patrons to commission family likenesses from artists of the caliber of Gainsborough and Reynolds. The portrait of Sir Jeffery Amherst is a prime example of the grand style; of Reynolds's unique blend of pose and characterization which owed more than a little to van Dyck and with which the first President of the Royal Academy flattered and immortalized his sitters. This is the legacy which Reynolds bequeathed to his successors, in such a way as to influence the subsequent mainstream of British portrait painting. As a result, to quote (Sir) Ellis Waterhouse, "English painting was to become, in the course of the next two decades, something much more solemn and portentous."[1] The immediate decade of which he was writing, the fifth of the eighteenth century, is precisely the one in which George Beare painted the portrait of an unidentified woman (fig. 1) which was acquired by the Mead Art Museum earlier this year.[2] This portrait in oils, which is neither solemn nor portentous, is an important example of English portrait painting before Reynolds, of portraiture which is "simple, unmannered and personal."[3]

The words were those used by C. H. Collins Baker, who published Beare as a re-discovery in 1958. The previous literature is scant; in 1878 Samuel Redgrave referred to a portrait by Beare of John, 4th Duke of Bedford (whereabouts unknown),[4] and in 1948 Waterhouse attributed to Beare a portrait of Sir John Wynn.[5] Today, the facts known about George Beare can still be stated in a single sentence. He painted in the western counties of England, probably based upon Salisbury, during the fifth decade of the eighteenth century. He survives less as an artistic personality than as a signature upon some twenty portraits, to which ten more have been added in the course of the last thirty years, on stylistic grounds.

Collins Baker did not have the advantage of knowing the Mead Museum portrait which did not appear on the London market until 1984.[6] Signed and dated 1748, it is an important addition to an œuvre which has begun to emerge from the artistic penumbra of William Hogarth, to whom more than one of Beare's masterpieces has been firmly mis-attributed. For Beare, like Hogarth, approached portraiture with straightforward, pictorial honesty. Our sitter is shown well-dressed, with a good deal of care taken to represent the precise fabrics and stuffs of her elaborate costume. Her dress is the material counterpart to the composure (and complacency) of her features. Devoid of any kind of movement or tension, this middle-aged gentlewoman is depicted without flattery, but sympathetically, and with that measure of psychological insight which explains the periodic confusion of Beare with Hogarth.

Beare's portrait of *Jane Coles as a child* (Ven House), was, as Waterhouse pointed out,[7] exhibited twice as the work of Hogarth before the evidence of the signature was insisted upon. The reason is plain; it is difficult to cite another painting of the same date to stand beside Hogarth's portrait of the *Graham children* of 1742 (Tate Gallery, London) or his *Lord Grey and Lady Mary West as Children* (which may be a fragment of a larger picture) in the Washington University Gallery of Art, St. Louis, Mo. We have only to compare the portrayal of children in these works by Hogarth and Beare with earlier representations of adults in miniature to recognize their respect for minors *per se*.[8] It emerges, once again, with unmistakable sympathy and clarity in the double portrait of an unidentified woman and child (fig. 2) in the Yale Center for British Art, which is signed and dated 1747. The subject in this outstanding example of Beare's art is unusual, insofar as it presumably portrays a grand-

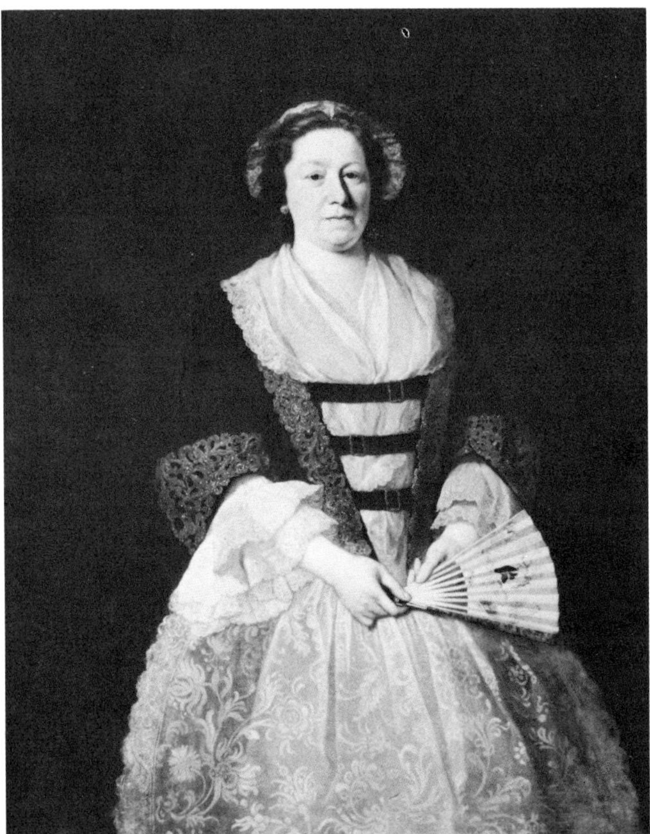

Fig. 1 George Beare (fl. 1741–1749)
English, 18th Century
Portrait of an Unknown Lady, 1747
Oil on canvas, 50 × 40"
Museum Purchase
1985.4

mother with her granddaughter. The characterization of both is sharp to the point of discomfort; the older woman stares outward, as uncompromised by her age as she is unflattered by her portrait, the protectress of the child at her side.

Like Hogarth's, Beare's sitters appear to have been professional people, merchants or members of the landed gentry (as opposed to the aristocracy). For instance, the two examples of his work which have found their way into the National Portrait Gallery in London are respectively of an architect *(Francis Price, 1747)* and a tractarian *(Thomas Chubb, 1747)*. His most formal surviving portrait is that of *Judge Charles Clarke* of 1745 (private collection, Wales). The greater number of Beare's subjects are unidentified, and will remain so, as men and women of substance in their own times, but lacking the prominence or distinction necessary to earn entries in the *Dictionary of National Biography*. The unidentified man (fig. 3) in the Tate Gallery, dated 1746, bears comparison with the one of the same date in the Yale Center for British Art and, for that matter, both artistically and socially with Hogarth's portraits of *George Arnold* (fig. 4) and his daughter *Frances Arnold* painted c.1740, now in the Fitzwilliam Museum, Cambridge.

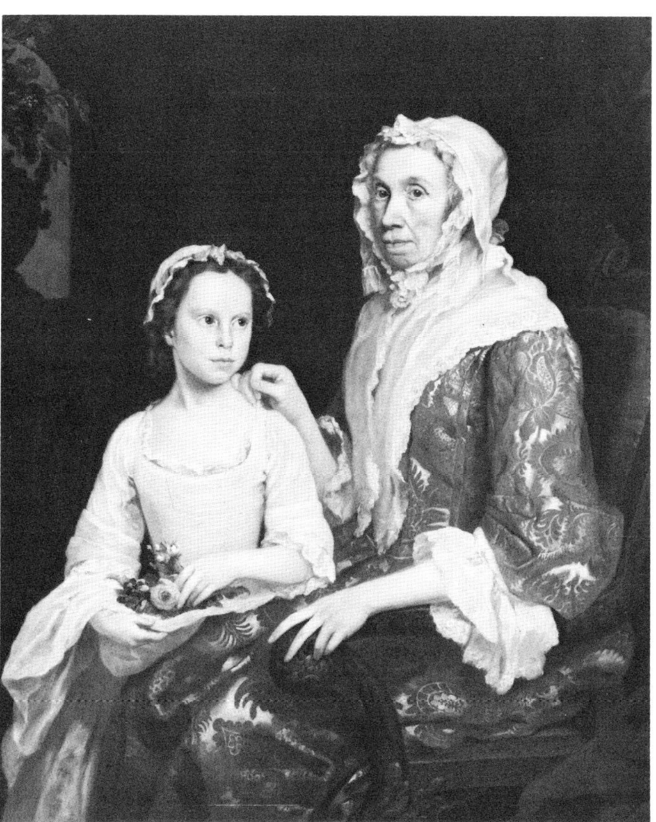

Fig. 2 George Beare (fl. 1741–1749)
  English, 18th Century
  Portrait of an Elderly Lady and a Young Girl, 1747
  Oil on canvas, 49¹⁄₁₆ × 40¼″
  Yale Center for British Art, Paul Mellon Collection
  B1976.7.180

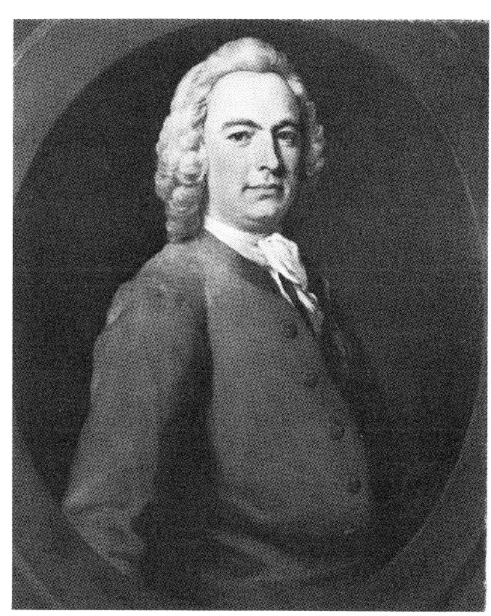

Fig. 3 George Beare (fl. 1741–1749)
  English, 18th Century
  Portrait of a Gentleman, 1746
  Oil on canvas, 30 × 25″
  The Tate Gallery, London

A comparison between Frances Arnold and the portrait tentatively identified as *Mrs. Ann Burney*, but firmly attributed to Beare (Kimbell Art Museum, Fort Worth, Texas) suggests that Beare was less inhibited about French influence than was his professionally xenophobic contemporary. Not that Hogarth himself was immune; as Antal showed,[9] his famous portrait of Captain Coram, which he presented to the Foundling Hospital in 1740, betrays a hidden debt to the portrait by Rigaud of Samuel Bernard which Hogarth could have seen in the engraving by Drevet. But whereas Hogarth resisted the influence of fashionable French painters, and of Jean-Baptiste van Loo especially when that artist established himself in London between 1737 and 1742, a glance at Beare's portrait of *Miss Fort of Alderbury House* (which is signed and dated 1747) reveals his susceptibility towards the rather coy theatricality which van Loo popularized in the society portrait. Both of these paintings by Beare, of Mrs. Ann Burney (?) and Miss Fort, share with the Mead Art Museum portrait a concern for the precise details of the sitters' dress. The same is true of the portrait of the unidentified woman (fig. 5) in the Worcester Art Museum, which is so close in costume to the Amherst picture that it is tempting to infer that the same dressmaker was involved! Seventy-five years ago the Worcester painting was bought as a work by Hogarth. It was relegated briefly to Highmore before Waterhouse recognized the hand of Beare. Both misattributions are relevant, for Highmore manifested a knowledge of French paintings as early as 1742, when he embarked upon his illustrations of Samuel Richardson's novel, *Pamela*. As Waterhouse has observed, these are indebted to Chardin, perhaps through engravings by Lepicié,[10] but they also indicate, with their impasto, an affection for those techniques of painting which can be learned only from canvas itself. Hogarth, Highmore, Beare and for that matter Hayman, that "meeting-place of two schools, the continental and the English":[11] perhaps the point to be made is that Beare shows the same artistic interests and preoccupations as his better known contemporaries. He may have operated in a provincial center, but, a sensitive barometer, he measured and reflected the major developments of the decade in which he worked.

In those lectures on three decades of British art from which I have quoted freely, Waterhouse contrasted Hogarth's "heroic, middle-class art" with what was to follow. To his American audience he proposed a link between the artistic trends of the third quarter of the eighteenth century and the political climate at the time of the Revolution; "a movement away from the honest style of Hogarth towards an arrogant and artificial style."[12] Whatever the validity of this particular line of enquiry, there is particular value in having George Beare's portrait in the Mead Art Museum, where it can also be seen in relation to early American painting. It reminds us of the transatlantic links which existed from 1728 onwards, when John Smibert set out for Bermuda as a member of Bishop Berkeley's expedition. More specifically, it demonstrates the continued appeal of the "simple, unmannered and personal" style, not only among patrons and painters in the English counties, but also among their contemporaries in the furthest of the artistic provinces, colonial America.

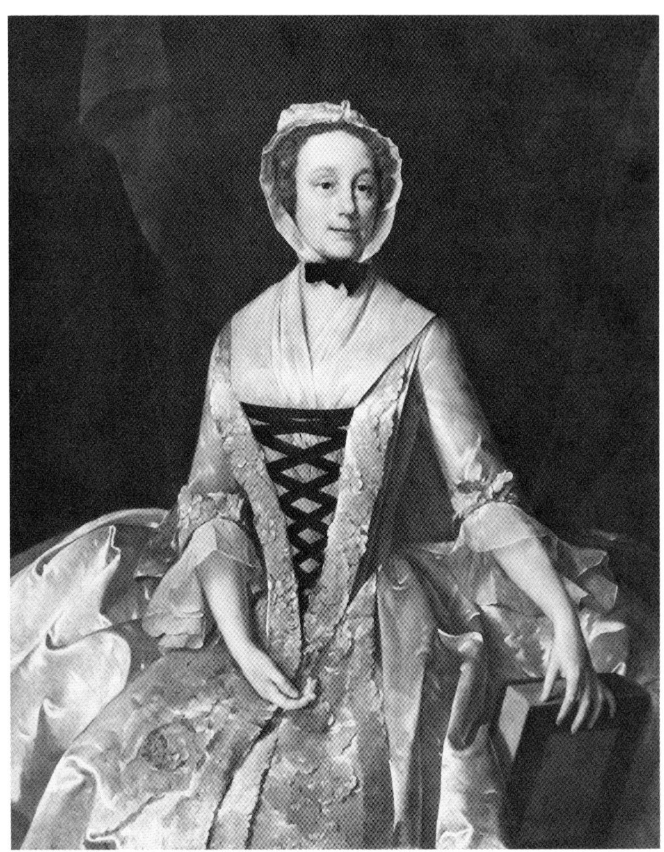

Fig. 5 George Beare (fl. 1741–1749)
English, 18th Century
An Unknown Lady
Oil on canvas, 49⅞ × 39⅞"
Worcester Art Museum
1910.9

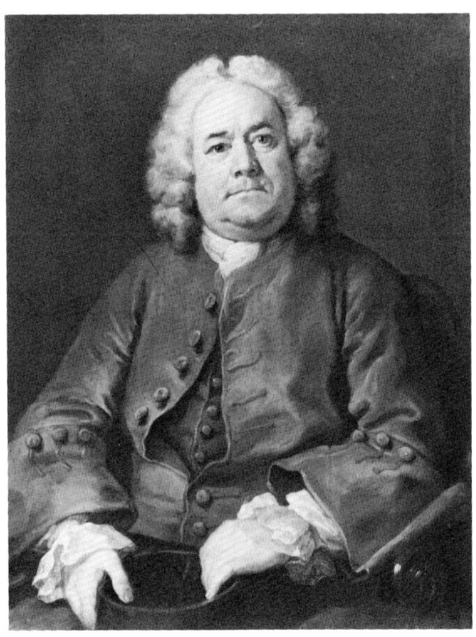

Fig. 4 William Hogarth (1697–1764)
English, 18th Century
George Arnold
Oil on canvas, 35 × 27"
Fitzwilliam Museum, Cambridge
No. 21

FOOTNOTES

1. Ellis Kirkham Waterhouse, *Three Decades of British Art 1740–1770*. Jayne Lectures for 1964, Philadelphia, American Philosophical Society, 1965, p. 12. This article was written prior to the death of Sir Ellis Waterhouse on September 7, 1985. Its debt to a pioneer of British art history is acknowledged passim; it is also dedicated to his memory.

2. *Portrait of an Unknown Lady*, oil on canvas, 50 × 40" (128 × 104 cm). signed and dated 1748. Mead Art Museum, Amherst College, 1985.4

3. C.H. Collins Baker, "A Portrait Painter Re-discovered," *Country Life*, 123, March 20, 1958, pp. 572–3

4. Samuel Redgrave, *A Dictionary of Artists of the English School*. London, 1894, p. 32

5. Waterhouse, "Portraits from Welsh Houses—The Exhibition at the National Museum of Wales," *Burlington Magazine*, XC, July 1948, pp. 203–7

6. The painting was sold at Phillips, London, December 11, 1984, lot 110. It was bought by the Mead Art Museum from Roy Miles, Fine Paintings, London.

7. Waterhouse, *Painting in Britain 1530 to 1790*, Harmondsworth: Penguin Books, 1953, p. 138; 4th (integrated) edition, 1978, p. 186

8. For changing attitudes towards children, see J.H. Plumb, "The New World of the Children in Eighteenth Century England," *Past and Present*, no. 67, 1975, pp. 65–95, and I. Pinchbeck and M. Hewitt, *Children and English Society*, I, 1969

9. Frederick Antal, "Hogarth and his borrowings," *The Art Bulletin*, 29, March 1947, pp. 36–48

10. Waterhouse, *Three Decades*, p. 4

11. T.S.R. Boase, in the *Journal of the Warburg and Courtauld Institutes*, X, 1947, p. 91

12. Waterhouse, *Three Decades*, author's preface, n.p.

HISTORY PAINTINGS AND THE NARRATIVE TRADITIONS
Frank Trapp

Although Britain was comparatively late in realizing a native school of painting, once given an appropriate climate of patronage and station, the artists of that land made contributions that have only recently gained adequate recognition abroad. Relationships with the American Colonies and later the United States, were for a time, of enormous importance on both sides of the Atlantic. As the nineteenth century progressed, sympathetic yet differentiated patterns of taste and expression evolved in those two locales. In the beginning, however, "Anglo-American" artists are necessarily to be accounted by historians concerned with the art of either nation, so that numerous major figures are best so identified.

The position of the enterprising Benjamin West (1738–1820), for example, who reigned for three decades as Second President of the Royal Academy, is indicative of those early convergences. If not the initiator of Neoclassicism in Britain—Gavin Hamilton had after all, preceded him to Rome and earlier explored the theories advanced by J.J. Winckelmann, Anton Raphael Mengs and their sympathizers—West seized upon their possibilities and exploited them more effectively. Largely through his aegis as a teacher and diplomat of the arts,

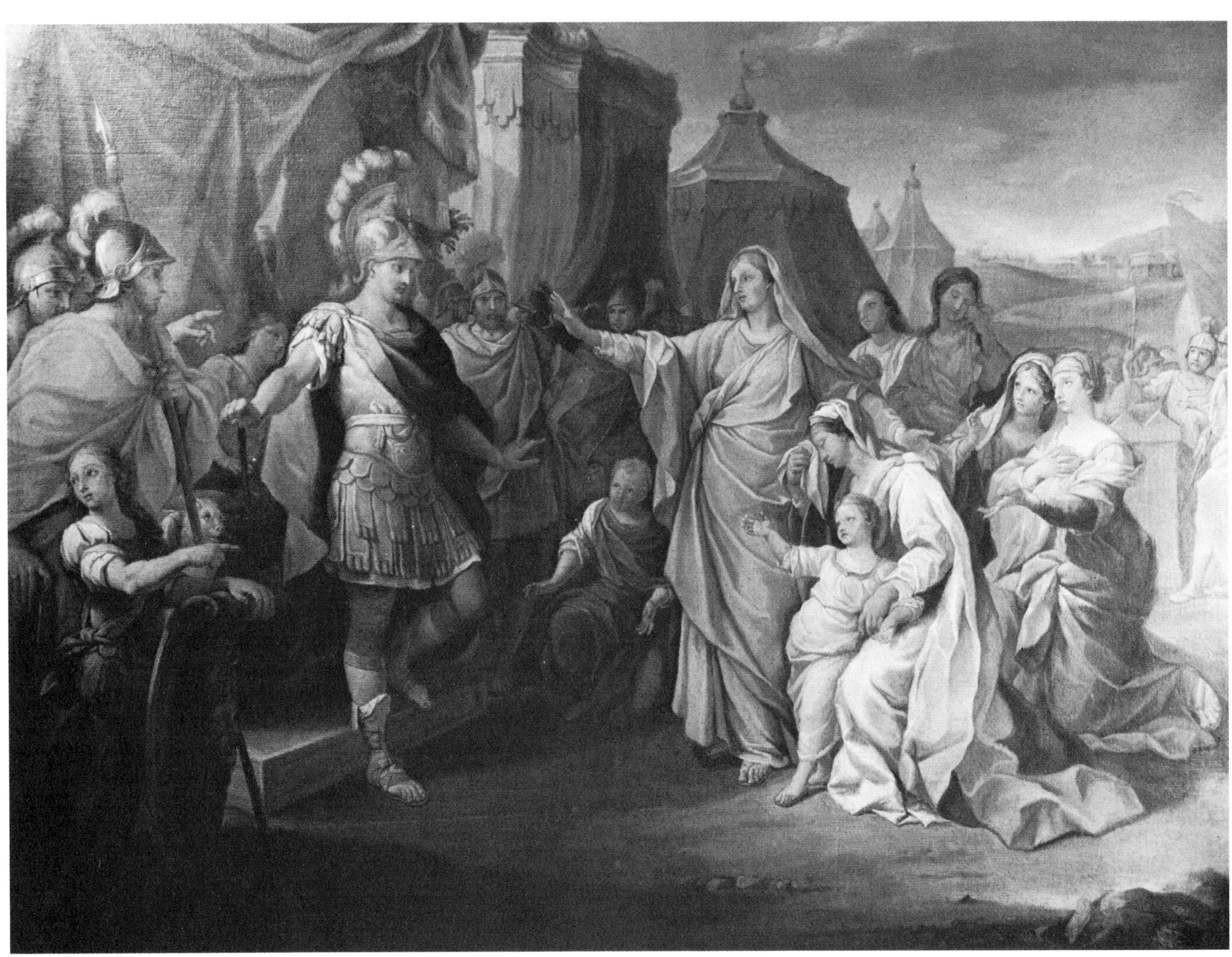

Fig. 1 Attributed to Benjamin West (1738–1820), or perhaps from the
circle of Agostino Masucci (ca. 1691–1758)
Coriolanus Yields to His Mother's Appeal
Oil on canvas, 1792, 39 × 52"
Museum Purchase
1961.91

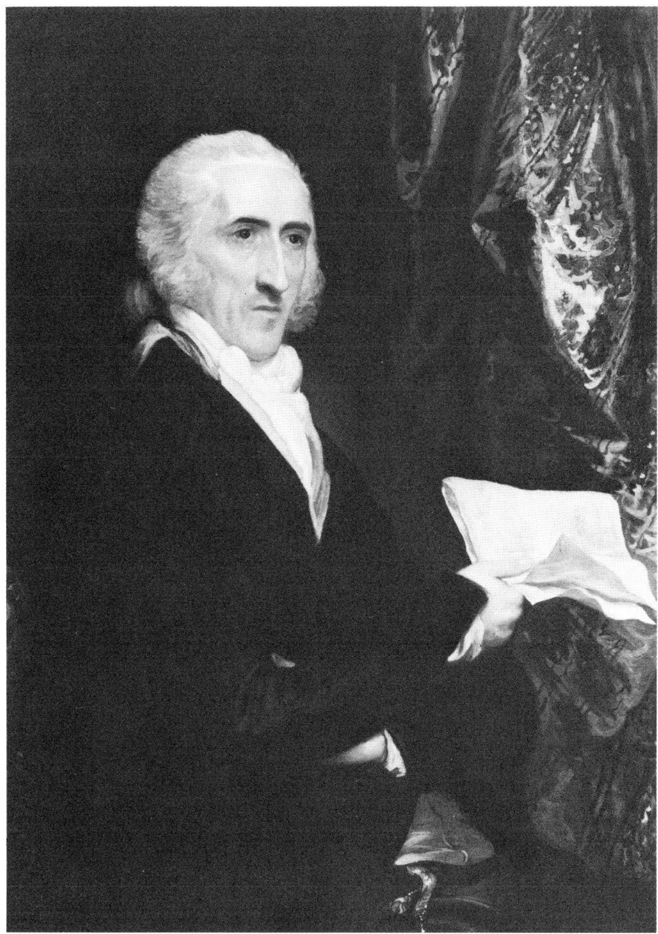

Fig. 2 Sir Benjamin West (1738–1820)
Portrait of Dr. Enoch Edwards (1751–1802), 1795
Oil on canvas, 36 × 28″
Gift of Herbert L. Pratt, '95
P1938.1

the Continent. Much the same can be said with regard to depictions of the novelties of a dawning Industrial Age (as with some of Joseph Wright of Derby's subjects). Closely related to these provocative disclosures was the British development of the so-called "conversation piece," in which genre painting and portraiture were fused, often very ingeniously, or the "fancy picture," in which Richard Parkes Bonington excelled, where historical personages were viewed in intimate moments which the mind's eye might conjure. Innovations of the kind were abundant if sometimes left unexploited within the British milieu—perhaps from the want of appropriate conditions of patronage. At any rate, the framework if not the full range of subtleties of these developments can be illustrated from within the contents of the Amherst College Collection. It may be hoped that the future will provide more amply in these areas.

West stood at the center of these complicated eddies of cultural identity. A painting long attributed to West, *Coriolanus Yields to His Mother's Appeal*, dated 1792, illustrates some of the questions aroused by his variability as an artist. This canvas (fig. 1) has recently been assigned to the Circle of Italian painter Agostino Mas-

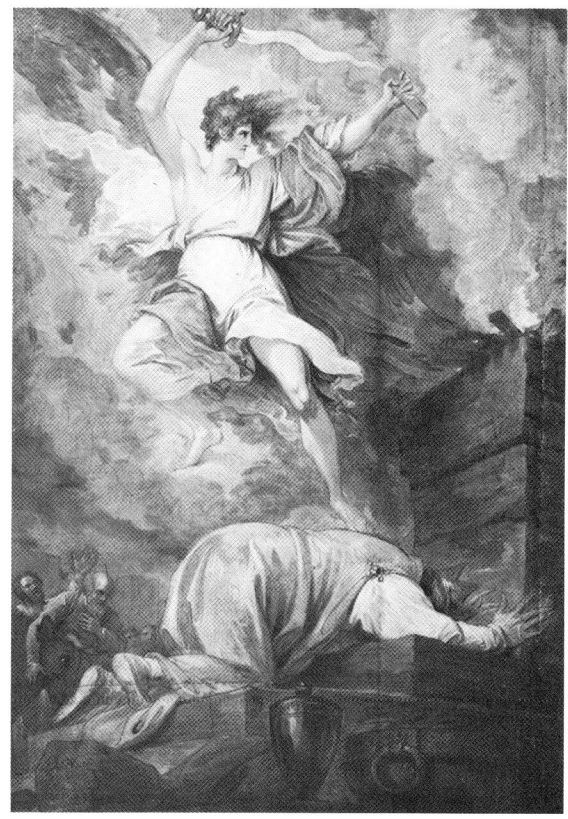

Fig. 3 Sir Benjamin West (1738–1820)
David Prostrate, Whilst the Destroying Angel Sheathes the Sword, 1798
Oil on paper, mounted on panel, 31 × 22″
Museum Purchase
1950.23

classical subjects and other forms of History Painting (scenes from recorded history or from religious or classical lore) took shape at the hands of many of West's younger contemporaries. Among them, such compatriots as John Singleton Copley or Washington Allston, both of whom enjoyed long periods of residence in England, made significant essays in that direction—one prescribed by Reynolds as the noblest, yet in some ways more a part of his theoretical discourse than of his professional practice.

Yet it is also the case that the Neoclassical penchants of the time were most fully realized slightly later and elsewhere, particularly in France, amongst the circle of Jacques-Louis David. Other precocious British based gestures such as rendering historical subjects in contemporaneous costume (as with Copley) or consorting with provocative Romantic effects (as with West and later, Fuseli and Blake), also assumed a more sustained momentum and a fuller measure of definition on ucci (1691/92–1758), or the related master Francesco Imperiali (flourished 1730), who had in fact begun a painting of Coriolanus which had been unfinished at the time of his death and was completed by Masucci in 1740.[1] Because the Amherst picture reflects a style of that early phase of Neo-classicism and is in other ways as well, anomalous within his œuvre, it has been proposed at a work by Masucci. On the other hand, close technical examination shows the signature and date appearing on the shield to be contemporaneous with the rest, and it seems somehow unlikely that West would have signed as his own a painting altogether by another hand. Or perhaps it is a student copy, done at a time when as a facile newcomer to the European scene, West cast his net wide, especially during and just after the period he spent in Rome, 1760–1763, on his lengthy trip from Philadelphia to London, where he would make his home. In the lack of definitive evidence to the contrary, this seems the most likely probability. Whatever the case, this impressive composition links with the emergence of a stricter Neoclassicism out of roots in the late Baroque. And whoever the author may have been, the composition surely looks forward to West's remarkable

and precocious essays in that vein, such as *Agrippina with the Ashes of Germanicus* (1767), now at Yale, and not backward, as the inscribed date of 1792 would somehow seem to imply. Hence, this tantalizing attributional question must for the time being be left moot.

Two other paintings far more securely identified with West here relate. His *Portrait of Dr. Enoch Edwards,* 1795 (fig. 2) requires notice for its remarkably different handling from that of the *Coriolanus.* While in Italy, West had been urged to study Titian. Lessons learned from the Venetians then or since are handsomely attested to in the Edwards portrait, most of all in the vibrantly colorful, loosely handled passages devoted to the drapery at the upper right. While West was stylistically elusive in his sometimes surprising, eclectic turns of manner, he was a freer and experienced master in the 1790's.

West's sometimes more painterly and Romantic inclinations—and here again, he was exceedingly precocious within the larger, European scene—are given Baroque urgency and force of invention in his oil study, *David Prostrate, Whilst the Destroying Angel Sheathes the Sword,* 1798 (fig. 3). It shows David repentent at the

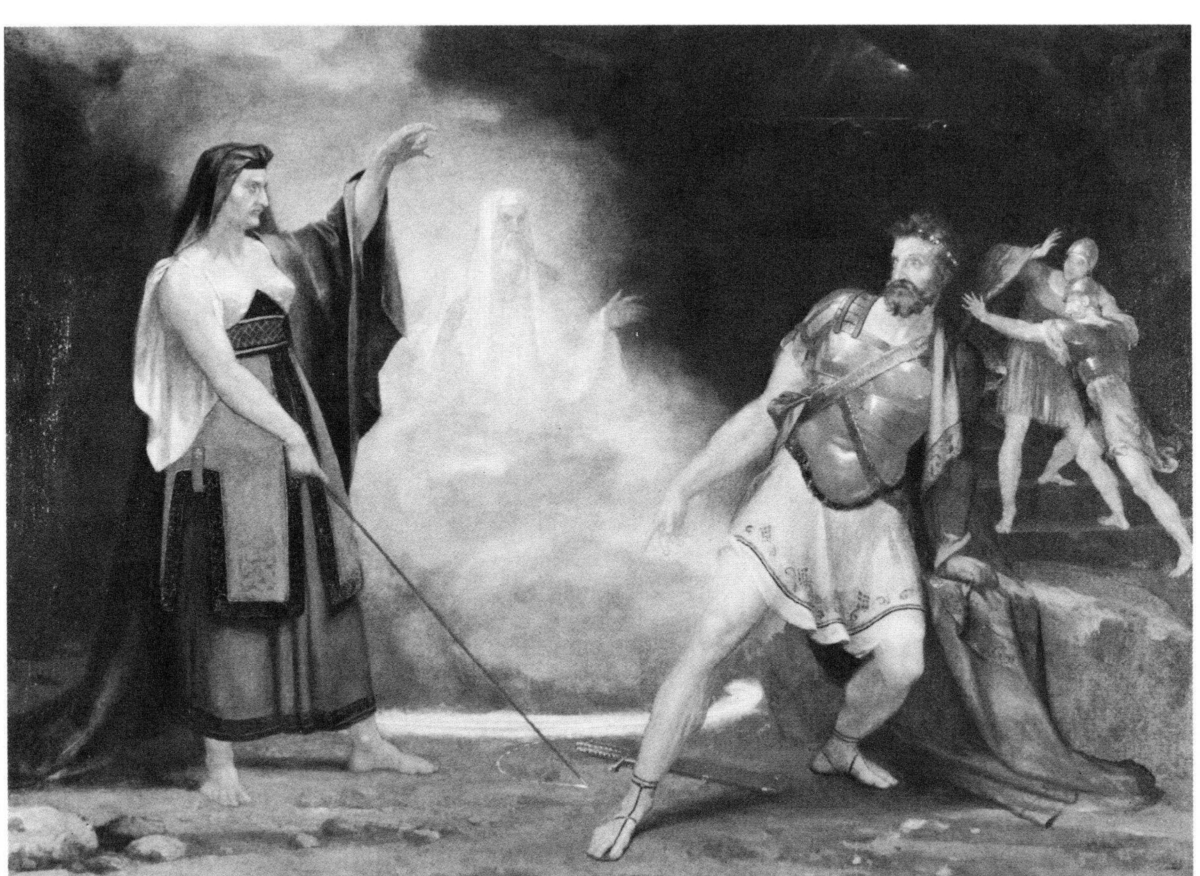

Fig. 4 Washington Allston (1779–1843)
   Saul and the Witch of Endor, 1820–21
   Oil on canvas, 34 × 47"
   Museum Purchase
   1947.96

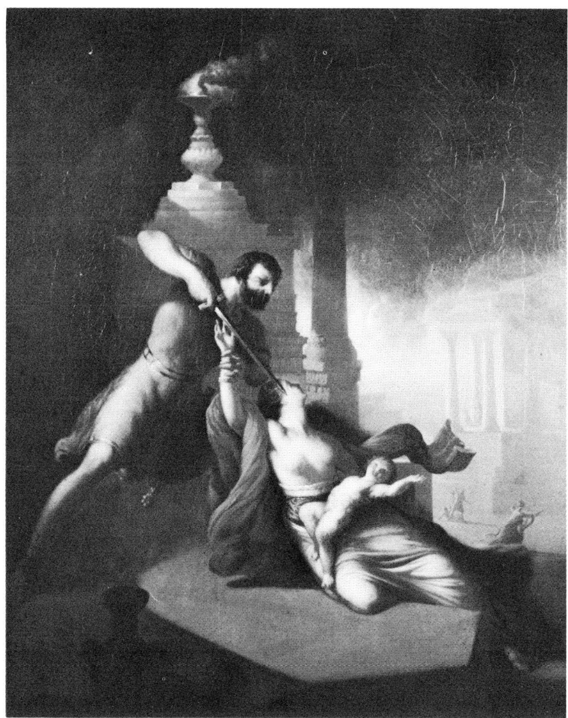

Fig. 5 Dr. William Rimmer (1816–1879)
  Massacre of the Innocents, ca. 1855–1861
  Oil on canvas, 27 × 22″
  Gift of Herbert W. Plimpton, The Hollis W. Plimpton '15
  Memorial Collection
  1973.92

freedom of handling, Allston's piece faithfully reflects the traditions of History painting encouraged at the Royal Academy and at the same time links with later reverberations of the Grand Manner as served on both sides of the Atlantic.

In this context it seems appropriate to mention the understandable confusion of two artists who bore the name, William Rimmer/Rimer. One of them (1816–79) the well-known Boston painter, sculptor, draughtsman, and physician, is represented in the Amherst College Collection by a *Massacre of the Innocents* (fig. 5), painted around 1855–1861 in the startlingly managed way characteristic of that remarkable individualist. *The Coronation of Queen Esther* (fig. 6a), once thought to be by Dr. Rimmer, is now thought likely to be instead the product of an English contemporary of a like name. That alteration of attribution would not only explain the striking differences of handling in the latter work, with its much more painterly technique, but also its tamer, more

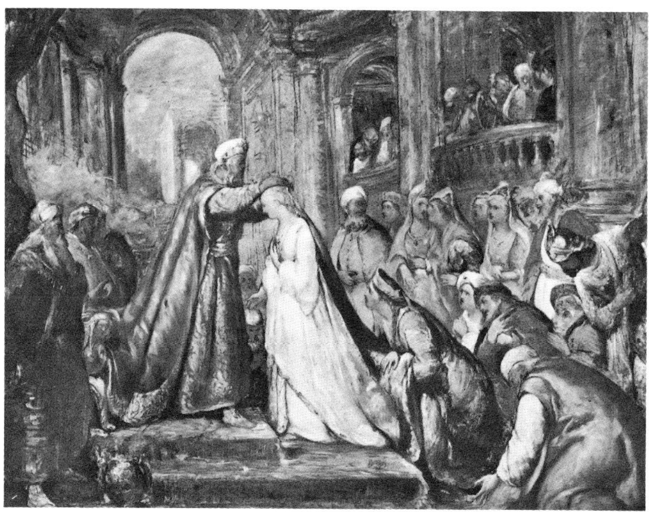

Fig. 6a William Rimer (?)
  The Coronation of Queen Esther, 1847
  Oil on panel, 19¾ × 26¼″
  Gift of Herbert W. Plimpton, The Hollis W. Plimpton '15
  Memorial Collection
  1973.91

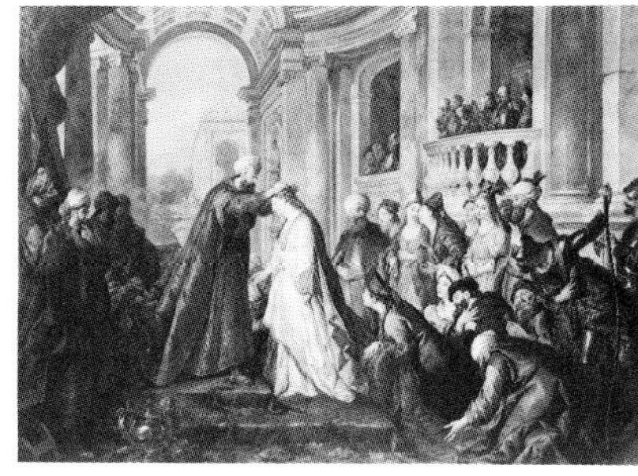

Fig. 6b Jean-François de Troy (1679–1752)
  Le coronnement d'Esther, 1737
  Oil on canvas, 10½′ × 15½′
  Musée du Louvre
  INV8213

altar (Samuel II. Ch. XXIV, 16–25), in the effort to spare Jerusalem from the destruction of an angry Lord. Perhaps done in preparation for a larger picture of much the same description, exhibited in 1800, this composition represents the growing popularity of biblical subjects at the time. The artist's sensitivity to the call of opportunity was surely a touchstone to his remarkable versatility as a performer.

West's countryman Washington Allston (1779–1843) later turned to a like essay, in which appears a subject earlier (in 1777) approached by West himself: *Saul and the Witch of Endor* (fig. 4). It represents an account given in Samuel I, Ch. 28, wherein Saul, fearful of the Phillistines, fails to recognize the spectre of the prophet, conjured by a witch to give him counsel. Although actually painted in his native Massachusetts, this composition was undertaken by Allston just after his return from his second, prolonged stay in England, where he was imbued with an ambition to work in the Grand Manner and a delight in the emotional provocation promised by the Sublime, a quality which enjoyed widespread appeal in that day. Full of the stagecraft and unabashed artifice admired at the time, the Mead Museum picture encapsulates the artistic qualities that won Allston a circle of ardent admirers in England, not the least of whom was Samuel Taylor Coleridge. Newly cleaned, to reveal an unexpected freshness of color and conventional composition. Under the circumstances, the fact that it is based on that of a cartoon by J.F. deTroy (fig. 6b) for a Gobelins tapestry in Windsor Castle no longer seems puzzling, as it once did.[3] So far, however, there is little published information about the English William Rimer, who seems to have been the author of the painting in question.

The classical associations which formed so important a part of History Painting are impressively attested in a remarkable oil study (fig. 7) by Thomas Barker (1769–1847) recently acquired for the Collection. Called "Barker of Bath," to avoid confusion with another artist of the same name, Barker's considerable reputation in his own day derived from his military subjects and his portraiture. Despite its uncharacteristic subject there is good reason to accept the attribution of this picture, quite aside from the posthumous inscription on the back of the canvas. As a young man of 21 Barker had begun a stay of four years in Rome, so he was imbued with the classical topography of Latium and familiar with the Gothic themes of grottoes and menacing *banditti* which had been popularized by Salvator Rosa and other, somewhat earlier Continental artists, in the rising tide of the Picturesque. He is said to have made sketches of the kind during his stay there. Moreover, the technique of the Amherst picture is considered consistent with that to be admired in other works securely documented as by Barker. Research on the subject matter itself remains somewhat inconclusive, however:

> *"The subject of the painting is not wholly clear: it belongs to the iconographical type of the blind beggar recognised as Belisarius by one of his former soldiers, or of Marius meditating amongst the ruins of Carthage: but the ruined Colosseum (unless intended merely as a form of visual shorthand for "Antiquity") is inappropriate to either, whilst the sketch lacks the begging-bowl pertinent to Belisarius, and the spectators would be an intrusion into the meditations of Marius."*
>
> *Report. Heim Gallery, London*

The application of the principles of the Grand Manner may be observed in yet another work representing the contribution of an Anglo-American artist, in this case, John Singleton Copley (1738–1815). While today Copley is generally admired as far the greatest American painter of his time, it should be noted that as a Boston Tory, he moved to England in 1774, hence before the American Revolution, and thus remained all his life a loyal subject of the Crown. Perhaps partly for that reason his works of the later, English period have not always been so much admired by American commentators as those remarkable portraits of his early years. In fairness, however, his continued development as an artist and his originality within those freshly assumed professional terms deserve full recognition. Indeed, his inventiveness within the genre of historical depiction was internationally significant in the introducton of appropriate, contemporary costume, where less specific chronological reference had previously sufficed.

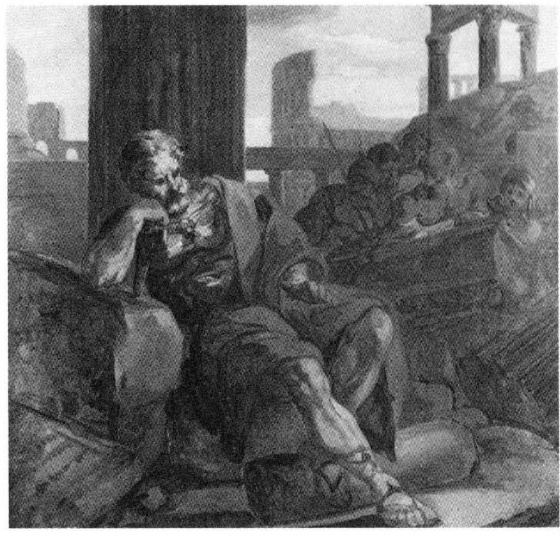

Fig. 7 Thomas Barker of Bath (1769–1847)
   Marius, ca. 1790–93
   Oil on paper laid on canvas, 19¼ × 19¾"
   Museum Purchase
   1984.15

Copley's *Death of Major Pierson,* was a landmark venture of the kind and it remains perhaps his most successful one. His *Death of Lord Chatham* (fig. 8) was also a significant contribution and in it, one may appreciate both the attractions and the limitations of the Grand Manner as a vehicle of historical representation. The powerful theatrics of the Baroque are apt to be too carefully choreographed for contemporary eyes, yet one can hardly help but admire their formal complexities. And while Copley, West, and others sought to capture a sense of immediate actuality in their stagings of these portentous events, their conceptual artifice was all too palpable, even to some of their alert fellows. The great David Garrick, for example, was reportedly unconvinced by some of the histrionics he observed enframed on the walls of the Royal Academy. Their conventions granted, however, these were works of imposing emotional as well as sheer physical proportion, and they link the grandiose achievements of the Baroque era with the *grandes machines* of the dawning nineteenth century.

Although Amherst's version of *The Death of Lord Chatham* has been relegated to the status of a copy[4], it affords a valuable sense of the intentions realized in the larger, authoritative version of the theme. Perhaps made as a studio record copy and almost certainly not as a preliminary study, this smaller replica of the subject approaches the quality one has come to expect of the master's own hand, especially in some of the portrait passages. At the very least it serves as a reminder—both in the subject itself and in the double nationality of the author of the composition—of the many ties to be accounted between artistic enterprises within the Anglo-American community of a former era.

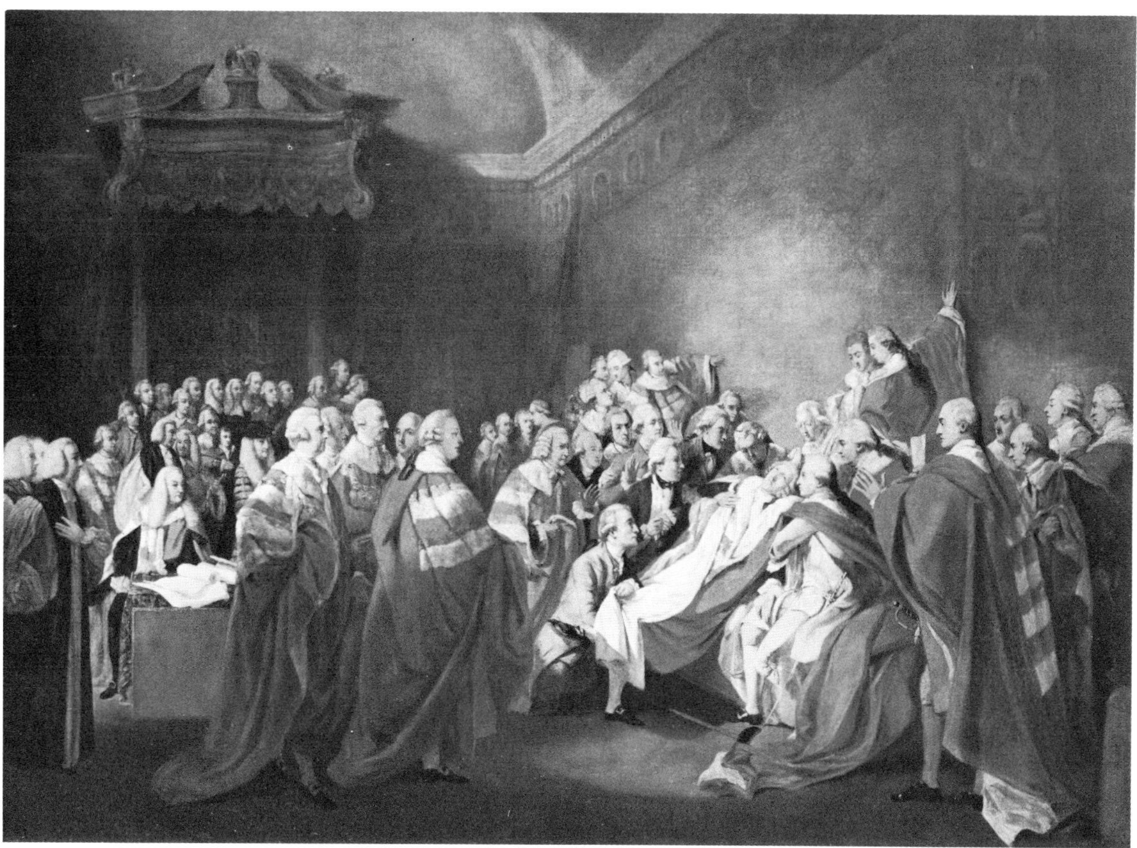

Fig. 8 Attributed to John Singleton Copley (1737–1815)
Death of the Earl of Chatham
Oil on canvas, 32 × 44⅛″
Bequest of Herbert L. Pratt, '95
1945.86

FOOTNOTES

1. This question is discussed in *American Art at Amherst, A Summary Catalogue of The Collection at the Mead Art Gallery Amherst College*, 1978, p. 209. The reattribution of the picture to Masucci was initiated by the late Anthony M. Clark. (See Mead Museum files, letter of February 26, 1963, from Clark to Charles H. Morgan). See also, Storrs, Conn., The William Benton Museum of Art, *The Academy of Europe, Rome in the 18th Century* (exhibition catalogue), pp. 55–56.

2. This source was pointed out by Prof. Jane Dillenberger. See *American Art at Amherst*, p. 177.

3. See, Palais de Tokyo, Paris, *Cahiers, Musée d'art et d'essai*, no. 17, *Jean-François de Troy: l'histoire d'Esther*. (Paris: Editions de la Réunion des musées nationaux, 1985). Special thanks are due to Mme Sylvie Beguin, Conservateur-en-chef at the Louvre, and to Mlle Marie-Catherine Sahut, organizer of the special exhibition treated in this monograph on De Troy's series of cartoon paintings, for the provision of the photograph of this particular subject and the authorization to reproduce it.

4. See, Jules David Prown, *John Singleton Copley*, 2 vols. (Cambridge, Massachusetts: Harvard U. Press, 1966), II, p. 437, note 3.

ANGELICA KAUFFMANN
by Judith A. Barter

A new addition to the holdings of British art at the Mead Art Museum is Angelica Kauffmann's *The Return of Telemachus* (ca. 1771–75). A fine example of Neoclassical History painting, it affords instructive comparisons with both earlier and later examples of allegorical and historical painting of the seventeenth through the nineteenth centuries.

Born in Switzerland, Angelica Kauffmann (1741–1807) subsequently lived in several parts of Italy before settling in Rome in 1763. The Rome to which she gravitated was an intellectually heady and cosmopolitan center. The renewed interest in Greek and Roman art, then at a crest, profoundly influenced its international company of artistic residents. Among them, the Scottish-born Gavin Hamilton (1723–98) had painted Homeric subjects during the 1760's and there were published books of engravings depicting "Etruscan" antiquities (see figure 1). Even earlier, in 1744, Giovanni Battista Piranesi (Venice 1720–1778) had settled in Rome, where he published his famous views of architectural ruins or "vedutte." The German-born librarian J.J. Wincklemann there published his first book, *History of the Arts*, in 1755, and he thenceforth continued to promote his adoration of "Greek" subject matter (which he knew entirely from literature) with a nearly religious fervor. When Kauffmann came to Rome she met Wincklemann almost immediately. The two adored each other, and under his influence she devoted herself to classical and allegorical compositions, working especially hard to improve her handling of architectural settings and perspective.[1] In 1764 she painted a portrait of her mentor, now in the Kunsthaus, Zurich.[2]

A person of parts, Kauffmann was an accomplished musician and amateur actress in addition to being a painter. Throughout her life, music and painting figured equally. Also gifted as a linguist, she spoke fluent Italian, German, French, and English. Considered both intelligent and charming by her contemporaries and moving easily in favored social circles, she became acquainted with many of the foreign tourists in Italy. In July, 1765 Kauffmann met Lady Wentworth, wife of John Murray, the British Ambassador. Because of this friendship and Kauffmann's awareness of the prospects of financial success on the London art market, she decided to go to England with her new patron. Evidence from Joseph Farington's famous dairy suggests that she may have also wanted to go to London because of her current flirtation with Nathaniel Dance (later Sir Nathaniel Holland), a fellow painter then studying in Rome. Whatever the reasons, Kauffmann actually did go to London in June 1766. There she formed friendships with another Swiss-born painter, Henry Fuseli, and with the eminent Sir Joshua Reynolds. Becoming popular almost overnight, she painted royal portraits in 1767. While her primary livelihood was gained from portrait commissions, she also exhibited numerous classical subjects at various London exhibitions.

Kauffmann's career as an exhibitor began with showings with the Free Society of Artists, where she exhibited classical subjects in 1765, 1766 and 1768. However, her attention was quickly turned to the newly formed Royal Academy. She was nominated for membership by Sir Joshua Reynolds. Zoffany's depiction of the membership (see figure 2) shows the two female founding members of the Academy, Kauffmann and Mary Moser, as portrait busts upon the wall to the right rather than as being actually present in the life-drawing class. Social mores of the time made it indecorous and inappropriate for women to draw from the male nude.

At the first exhibition of the Royal Academy (1769) Kauffman showed four classical subjects. One depicted Penelope taking down the bow of Ulysses for the contest of her wooers. In 1770 and 1771, she sent further pictures with a subject drawn from the Odyssey, *The Return of*

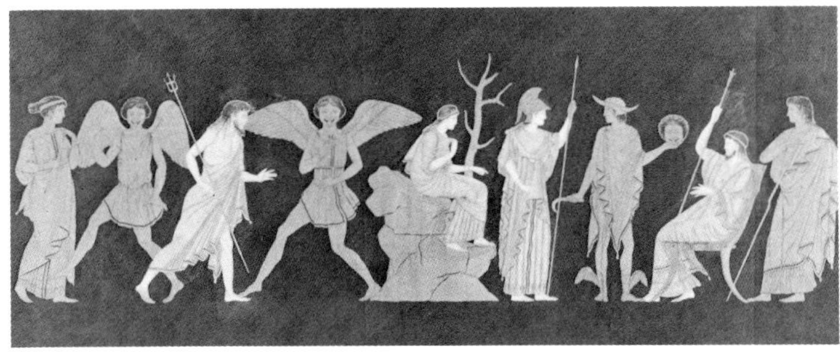

Fig. 1 Pierre François Hugues (1719–1805), Baron d'Hancarville
Plate From *Antiquités Etrusques, Grecques, et Romains, Tirées du Cabinet de M. Hamilton*
Hand colored etching, No. v. 4, 120; 18⅝ × 30″
Museum Purchase
1981.64

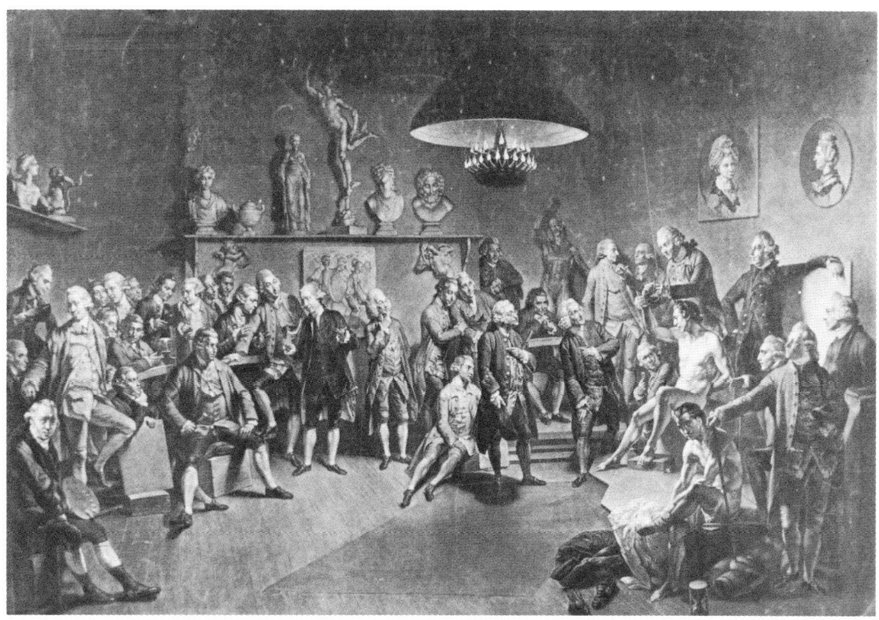

Fig. 2 Richard Earlom (1743–1822) after Johann
    Zoffany (1733–1810)
    The Royal Academy, 1773
    Mezzotint engraving, 20¼ × 29″
    Museum Purchase
    1947.116

Telemachus. She exhibited another picture depicting the adventures of Telemachus *("Telemachus at the Court of Sparta")* in 1773, while the following year she exhibited *"Penelope invoking Minerva for the Safe Return of Telemachus."* In 1775 she showed ten pictures at the Royal Academy Exhibition (invoking the ire of fellow members), one of which was entitled, *"The Return of Telemachus,"*—an entry which Horace Walpole reportedly disliked.[3]

The *Return of Telemachus* painted by Kauffmann in 1771 was recorded in Charles Brandoin's (1733–1807) watercolor, *The Exhibition Room of the Royal Academy, in 1771,* now in the collection of the Huntington Library and Art Gallery, San Marino, California. Richard Earlom engraved this particular scene (fig. 3).[4] Kauffmann's picture is at the lower right of the engraving—near the lower center of the wall. One can make out the bending figures of Penelope and Telemachus and the outstretched arms of Eurycleia. Amherst's picture (fig. 4a) is one of several known renditions of this composition. Two others are at the Chrysler Museum, Norfolk, Virginia (fig. 4b) and at the Toledo Art Museum, Toledo, Ohio (fig. 4c). A fourth version, a *sopra porta,* was recorded in 1924 in the collection of the Earl of Derby, Knowsley.[5]

Kauffmann's penchant for painting scenes from Homer is certainly in keeping with eighteenth-century Neoclassical taste. The Homeric revival of this period championed the *Iliad* and the *Odyssey,* as the products of a culture at its peak of genius and moral purity, just before its collapse into a corruption and decay resulting from the artificialities of civilization.

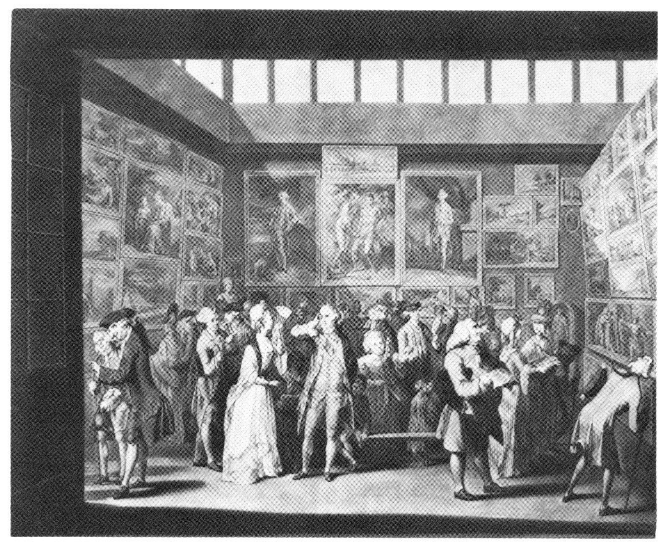

Fig. 3 Richard Earlom (1743–1822) after C. Brandoin
    *The Exhibition of the Royal Academy of
    Painting 1771*
    Mezzotint, 18½ × 22″
    Yale Center for British Art, Paul Mellon
    Collection
    B1978.43.798

Robert Wood's Essay on the "Original Genius and Writings of Homer" (1769) maintained that "while manners were rude, when arts were little cultivated and before science was reduced to general principles, poetry had acquired a greater degree of perfection than it has ever since obtained."[6] The image of the noble and pure appealed to the stoic side of the Neoclassical mentality, wherein the starkly tragic literature of the Greeks became the perfect vehicle for the virtuous humanism of the period.

Integral to the Homeric theme, the cult of Telemachus was a significant variation. The first book on Telemachus as a hero, written by François de Salignac, called Fénélon, appeared in 1699. It continued to be published throughout the eighteenth and nineteenth centuries.[7] Fénélon's book, with its elaborated and enhanced description of Telemachus' adventures in search of his father, was regarded by some as to be a satire of French court life.

Kauffmann's rendition of *The Return of Telemachus* more traditionally follows Homer's description in Book XVII of the *Odyssey*. In it, Telemachus, having found his father, leaves Odysseus to return to his mother, Penelope. Leaving his spear outside his mother's house, he steps across the threshold. The first to recognize him is Eurycleia, his aged nurse who runs to him, while the other household maids gather around. The beautiful Penelope emerges from her chamber and mother and son embrace in tender reunion.

Kauffmann's use of the Telemachus-Penelope subject serves as an indicator for several themes poular with Neoclassical painters. While Penelope was not technically a widow, the absence of her husband, the uncertainty of his safety, and her loyalty to him made her a figure in mourning and, in terms of the time, of virtue. The image of the grieving widow was a popular one—painted among others by Gavin Hamilton (1761) and

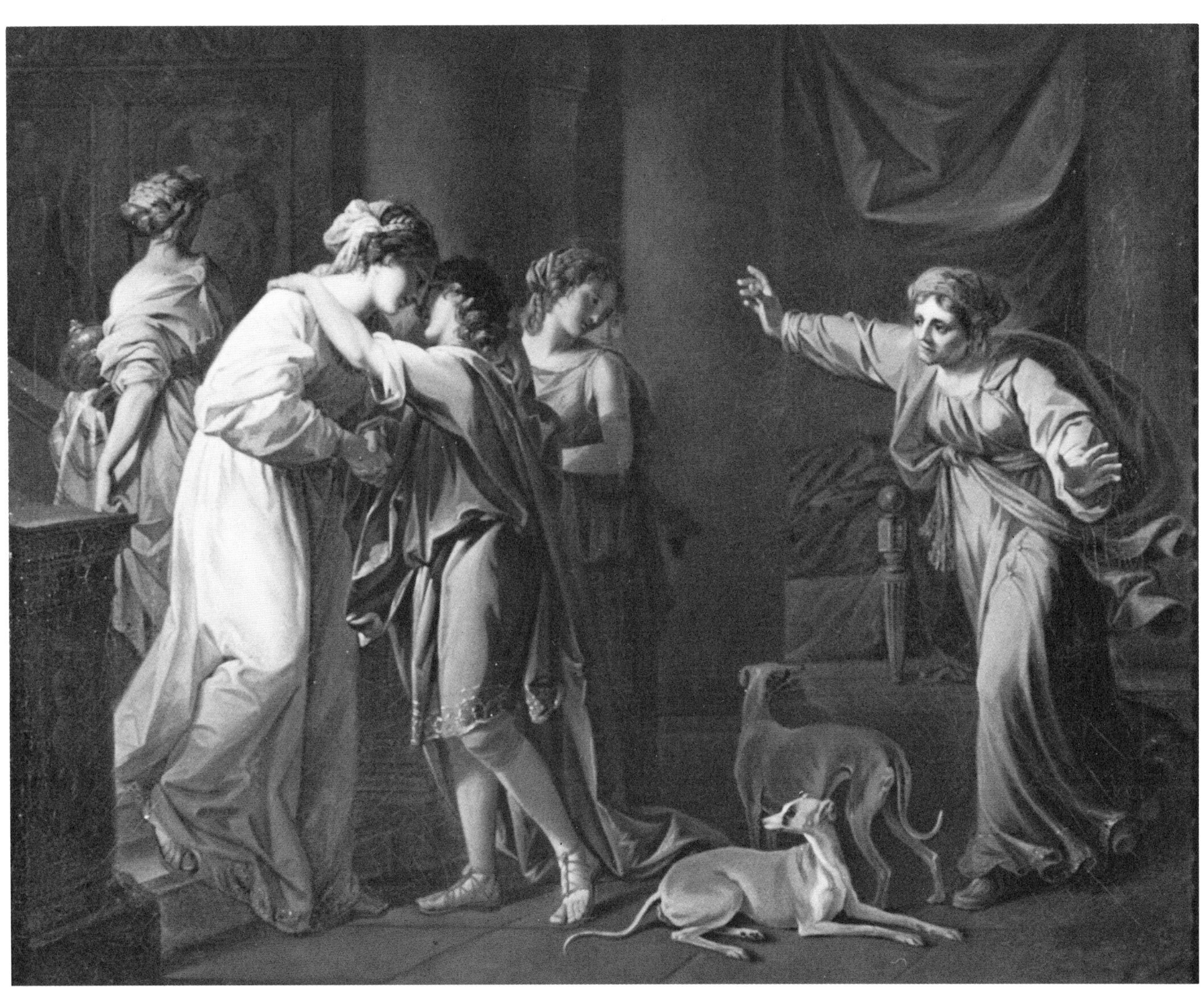

Fig. 4a Angelica Kauffmann (1741–1807)
    The Return of Telemachus, ca. 1770–80
    Oil on canvas, 46 × 56″
    Museum Purchase
    1984.91

later by J.-L. David (1783), who chose Andromache, the celebrated widow of Hector, as his subject. Kauffmann also painted an Andromache for exhibition at the Royal Academy in 1772. Benjamin West was among the first to illustrate the loyalty of the stoic widow and the fatalistic, dignified acceptance of tragedy as a subject for his famous rendition of *Agrippina with the Ashes of Germanicus* (1767).[8] All of these pictures share the celebration of a tragic moment faced with melancholy, grace, courage and stoicism. Beyond the virtuous message, the theme of womanly grief allowed the artist to select the most ideal or "perfect" attributes of feminine beauty of the day. Rosenblum points out the similarities between the pathos of Mary and her Lamentation and these secular renditions of grieving widows of antiquity.[9] Likewise, the figure of Telemachus returning after his wanderings, having departed initially without his mother's blessing yet received by her with love, is strikingly parallel to the story of the Prodigal Son. In the end, the separation of the family is healed and filial devotion restored.

In subjects such as this the didactic and moralizing intent associated with the Neoclassical movement is really Christian, with meanings cloaked in the iconographical garments of Greek and Roman history. Neoclassicism was thus not simply a change in taste from the rococo curls, shells and cupids, but an intellectual movement which revived the espoused moral superiority of neo-platonic idealism and attempted to use the themes of ancient history and literature to illustrate what contemporary society should be.

Kauffmann's painting drew some adverse criticism from her contemporaries. According to Farington, her friend Fuseli regarded the forms of her male and female figures as unduly idealized, too alluringly graceful and overly emotional.[10] Farington reported that Hoppner disliked her work and agreed with Pasquin that her drawing was more graceful than truthful. Pasquin recognized, however, that societal restrictions and ideas of delicacy had doubtless prevented her from ever drawing from the nude figure in the manner in which her male counterparts were trained. The dogs in the composition

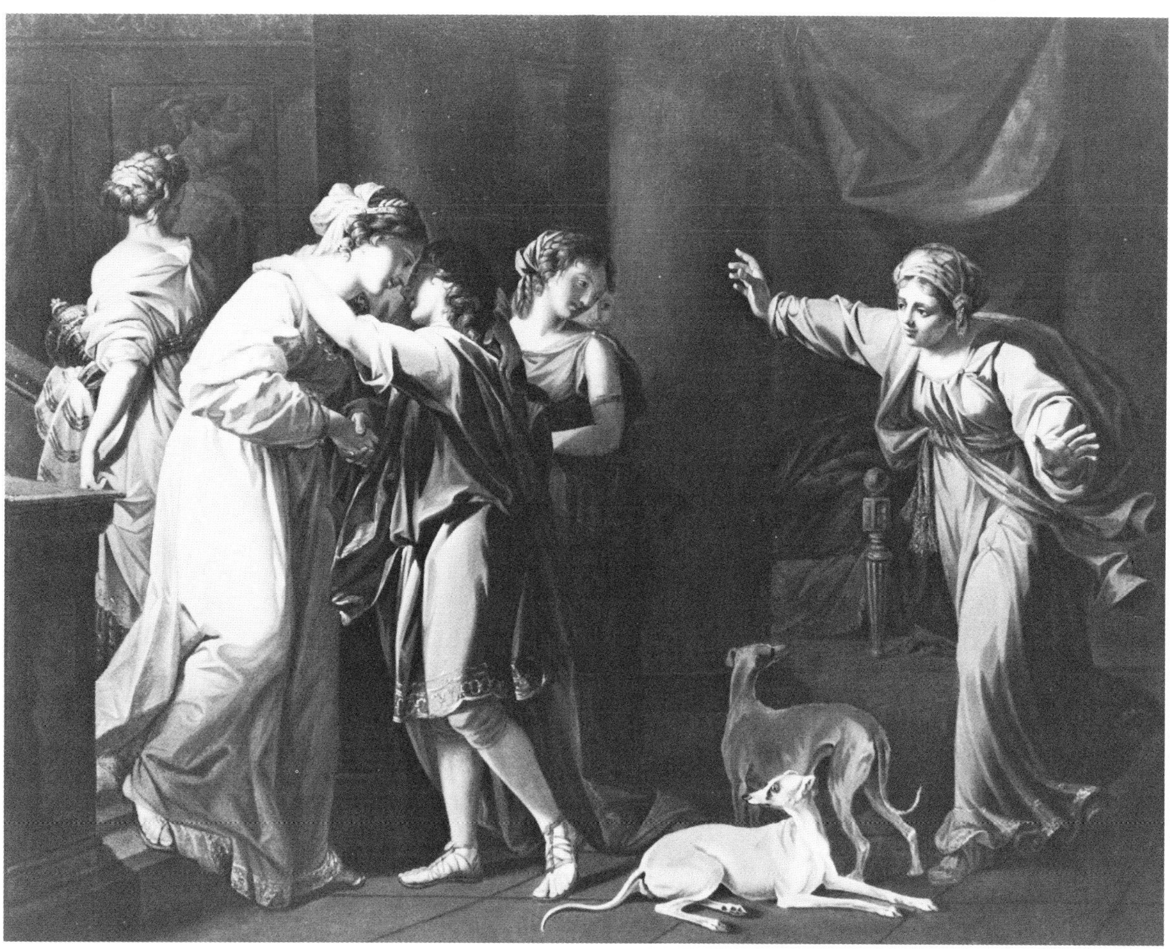

Fig. 4b Angelica Kauffmann (1741–1807)
  Telemachus Returning to Penelope
  Oil on canvas, 38 × 48½″
  The Chrysler Museum, Norfolk, VA, Gift of Walter P.
  Chrysler, Jr.
  71.665

remind the viewer of the decorative portraits of her Roman teacher, Pompeo Battoni, who was then extremely popular with English sitters. (See illustration elsewhere in the present volume.)

Kauffman's sense of rich, Venetian-like coloring, *transparent brushwork*, and sense of composition were much admired by her contemporaries. Her depiction of the classicised interior is skillful. Her figures are lined up in a frontal fashion which echoes the *trompe l'oeil* bas relief in the background, and allude to the groupings of figures found in ancient art, so successfully emulated by Wedgwood (fig. 5). The drawing is linear in the manner which we have come to associate with Neoclassical art. Curiously, what appears to modern eyes to be restrained to the point of artificiality, was criticized in its own day as overly emotional.

A few years after this picture was painted, Kauffmann married the painter Antonio Zucchi. The couple moved to Italy in 1780, returning to Rome at the height of its modern artistic vitality. The French Academy in Rome nurtured artists such as Jacques-Louis David, whose early masterpiece, *The Oath of the Horatii*, was painted there during the year 1784. Antonio Canova's funerary monument to Pope Clement XIV at the church of Santi Apostoli, Rome, was sculpted during 1783–7.

Thereafter, Kauffmann worked for the royal families of Naples and Rome but she continued to send pictures to exhibitions at the Royal Academy in London. In due course, she became a close friend of both Goethe and Canova. Goethe himself read his just finished *Iphigenia in Taurus* to her before anyone else, and Canova sculpted a portrait bust of the painter a month before her death.[11]

Still popular in London, her work was solicited for the famous Boydell Shakespeare Gallery. John Boydell

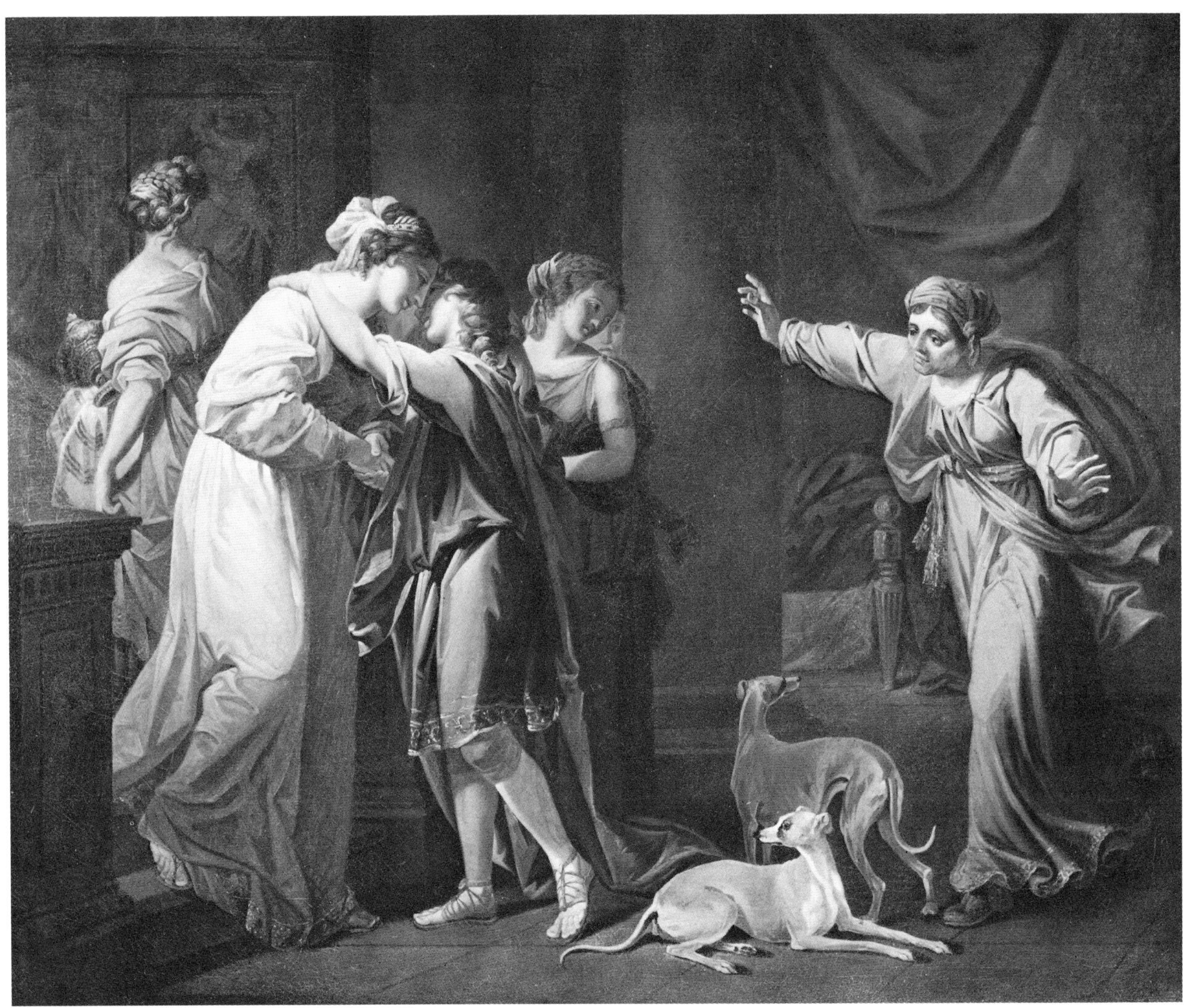

Fig. 4c Angelica Kauffmann (1741–1807)
The Return of Telemachus, ca. 1770–81
Oil on canvas, 39⅝ × 49¾"
The Toledo Museum of Art, Gift of
Edward A. Filene, Boston
38.24

(1719–1804), a print publisher and internationally known dealer, owned a gallery which commissioned scenes from Shakespeare by contemporary artists. Plates were engraved for sale after these pictures and distributed by subscription. Opened in 1789, by the time of its demise in 1803, the gallery possessed about one hundred and seventy pictures. Intense nationalism, belief in the importance of History painting and dedication to seeing this form of representation flower in Britain motivated Boydell. His inclusion of Kauffmann's work, even after she had returned to Italy, demonstrates that she was considered a British patriot. Indeed, as she continued to exhibit at the Royal Academy, her work was engraved by William Wynne Ryland, Francesco Bartolozzi and Thomas Burke (fig. 6). In all, her compositions were engraved over six hundred times, and her designs were used on fans, Worcester porcelain, painted furniture and other forms of the decorative arts.[12]

Ironically, because Kauffmann's work was so widely reproduced and the images so familiar to late eighteenth and early nineteenth-century audiences, interest in her efforts waned, and her reputation suffered severe neglect after her death in 1807. Scholarly attention to her work revived only in recent years of the present century. She deserves that special notice, for she was a brilliant, accomplished and worldly woman, one who maintained

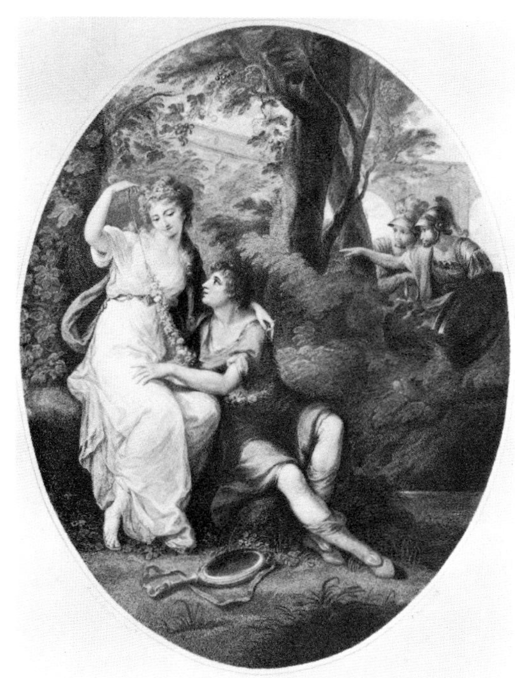

Fig. 6 Thomas Burke (1749–1815)
Rinaldo and Armida, 1795
Stipple engraving in colors, 13 × 10½"
From the Estate of Isabel J. Turner
1951.69

her independence and respected niche in a male workplace throughout a productive life, so that her studio also served as a well-known salon. As a first-rate colorist she brought to Britain a luminous, rich, yet less ponderous form of Neoclassicism than her British contemporaries generally espoused. And at an early date, along with Benjamin West, she can share the credit for formulating the standards of Neoclassical painting that soon came to assume prominence in the artistic production of Britain.

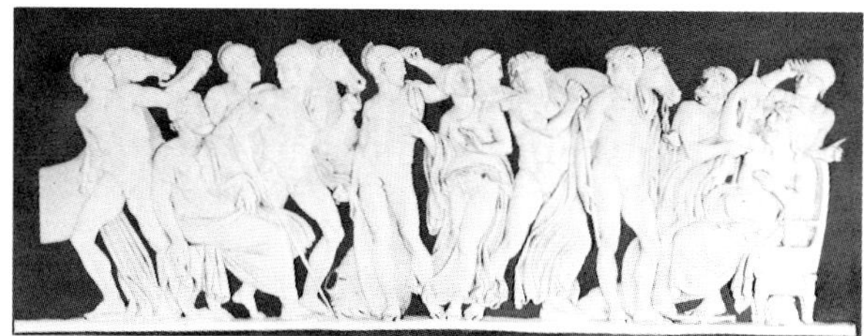

Fig. 5 English, early 19th Century
Wedgwood Plaque
6½ × 16½"
Gift of Mrs. Winifred L. Arms
1984.171

FOOTNOTES

1. Lady Victoria Manners and Dr. G.C. Williamson, *Angelica Kauffmann, R. A.: Her Life and Her Works*, (New York: Hacker Art Books, 1976), pp. 14–15.

2. Dorothy Moulton Mayer, *Angelica Kauffmann, R.A.*, (Gerrardo Cross, Buckinghamshire, England: Colin Smythe, 1972), pp. 31–32.

3. Manners and Williamson, pp. 236–237.

4. I am indebted to Kerry Sullivan of the Yale Center for British Art photographic archive for locating the watercolor and the engraving.

5. Manners and Williamson, p. 185.

6. Hugh Honour, *Neo-Classicism*, (Harmondsworth, Middlesex, England: Penguin Books, Ltd., 1968), p. 64.

7. Margaret R. Scherer, *The Legends of Troy in Art and Literature*, (London: Phaidon Press, 1963), pp. 179–180.

8. Robert Rosenblum, *Transformations in Late Eighteenth Century Art*, (Princeton, New Jersey: Princeton University Press, 1967), pp. 41–43.

9. Rosenblum, p. 29.

10. Mayer, p. 89.

11. Mayer, p. 183.

12. Germaine Greer, *The Obstacle Race*, (New York: Straus Giroux, 1979), p. 80.

THE PICTURESQUE, SUBLIME AND BEAUTIFUL
by Judith A. Barter

Volumes have been written regarding the eighteenth-century movement called the Picturesque and aesthetic attitudes toward nature and landscape painting. The purpose of this short article is not to recapitulate the complex interpretations or history of those aesthetics, but briefly to illustrate some examples of British eighteenth- and nineteenth-century landscape painting in the Mead collection with an eye to what they can teach us about the Picturesque and its related concepts of the Sublime and the Beautiful.

One of the most important essays on this topic was Edmund Burke's 1757 work entitled, *Philosophical Enquiry into the Origin of our Ideas of the Sublime and Beautiful*. In this essay Burke tried to define the elements necessary in a work of art to beget those emotions in the observer. The ingredients required to produce the passion caused by the Sublime included terror, obscurity, power, deprivation (such as solitude or silence), vastness or an infinity producing awe, and ultimately, pain. All of these qualities are anticlassical in nature and underlie the movement toward the full blown Romanticism of the nineteenth century. Burke's ideas about the passion of the Sublime are aptly illustrated by Philippe Jacques de Loutherbourg's painting which was exhibited at the Royal Academy (1804), *Landscape With Carriage in a Storm* (fig. 1). In it the forces of nature and of circumstance or fate are unleashed in a terrifying manner which evokes the contemplation of the Sublime as Burke described it:

"No passion so effectually robs the mind of all its powers of acting and reasoning as fear. For fear being an apprehension of pain or death, it operates in a manner that resembles actual pain. Whatever therefore is terrible, with regard to sight, is sublime

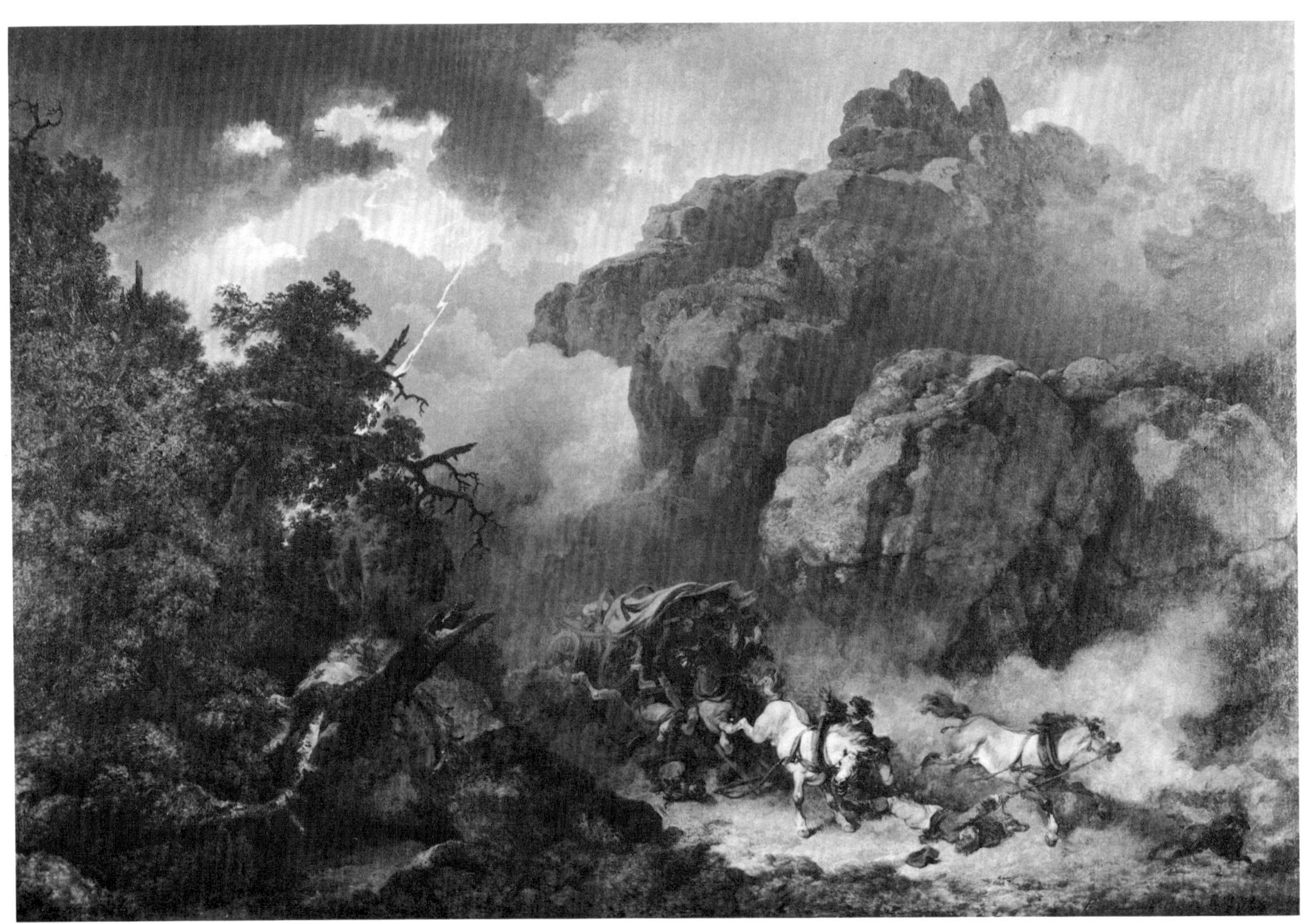

Fig. 1 Philippe Jacques de Loutherbourg (1740–1812), R.A.
   Landscape with Carriage in a Storm, 1804
   Oil on canvas, 28⅜ × 41½″
   Museum Purchase in honor of Susan Dwight Bliss
   1974.30

too, whether this cause of terror be endued with greatness of dimensions or not; for it is impossible to look on anything as trifling or contemptible, that may be dangerous." (PART II, sec. 2)[1]

While a painting of relatively average physical dimension, Loutherbourg's picture addresses the large-scale issues of fear, terror, pain and death. These themes arouse the passion of the Sublime. Technically, the anti-classical qualities of the painting are present in the asymmetry of composition, irregular, dramatic contrasts of light and shade, ruggedly painterly texture and a sense of motion. Like Salvator Rosa or Claude Vernet, whose works were widely favored at the time, Loutherbourg focussed his work on storms, avalanches, shipwrecks and other disasters that were sure to inspire thoughts of terror and astonishment, but which also lent themselves to the Picturesque formula of irregularity and extreme variety. Indeed, in works such as this one, Loutherbourg teetered on the edge of overt theatricism.

A native of Strasbourg, Loutherbourg came to London as a scenic artist and set designer for David Garrick. Loutherbourg's work is today considered to be precursory to the Romantic age which followed. His work was much admired by J.M.W. Turner during the first decade of the nineteenth century. While Turner, too, exhibited such subjects as avalanches, waterfalls and other dramatic and Sublime subjects, his work quickly surpassed that of Loutherbourg because it went beyond the more mechanical, theatrical, descriptions of Loutherbourg and conveyed more powerfully and first-hand the artist's emotional response to the natural world.

The exploration of the Sublime in landscape continued throughout nineteenth-century Romantic painting. In the work of Edward Lear (1812–1888) themes of the Sublime blended with Victorian topographical landscape painting. Lear is perhaps best known for the famous *Nonsense Books*, and imaginary beings such as the Owl and the Pussycat, but he was also a zoologist and painter of note. During the 1830's and 1840's he travelled extensively. *Views of Rome and its Environs* was published in 1841, followed by two illustrated travel books: *Journal of a Landscape Painter in Greece and Albania*, and *Journal of a Landscape Painter in Southern Calabria*. It is from the last volume that the Mead picture *Pentedatilo* is drawn.

At the time of Lear's travels (1847–48) Calabria was still a remote, strange and exotic place—fit subject for both topographical reporting and Sublime, visionary interpretations of the landscape. Lear described the landscape thus:

"Off we set; our route followed a tiresome and tortuous road in the bed of the Alice, and then became a rugged path crossing to the Fiume della Monaca ere Pentedatilo was visible; for this strange town is so placed, that although seen from all the country around, you may pass close to it without being aware of its proximity. The ravine in which the river flows is crowded and blocked up with crags to the south of the great rock on which the town is built; so that it is necessary to cross to the western side of the stream, and ascend the heights which enclose it before finally recrossing it, in order to reach the remarkable crag itself. But having gained the high ground opposite, the appearance of Pentedatilo is perfectly magical, and repays whatever trouble the effort to reach it may so far have cost. Wild spires of stone shoot up into the air, barren and clearly defined, in the form (as its name implies) of a gigantic hand against the sky, and in the crevices and holes of this fearfully savage pyramid the houses of Pentedatilo are wedged, while darkness and terror brood over all the abyss around this, the strangest of human abodes. Again, a descent to the river, and all traces of the place are gone; and it is not till after repassing the stream, and performing a weary climb on the farther side, that the stupendous and amazing precipice is reached; the habitations on its surface now consist of little more than a small village, though the remains of a large castle and extensive ruins of buildings are marks of Pentedatilo having once seen better days.

I had left Ciccio and the horse below at the stream, and I regretted having done so, when, as I sate making a drawing of the town, the whole population bristled on wall and window, and the few women who passed me on their way to the hanging vineyards, which fringe the cliffs low down by the edge of the river, screamed aloud on seeing me, and rushed back to their rocky fastnesses. As it is hardly possible to make these people understand ordinary Italian, a stranger might, if alone, be awkwardly situated in the event of any misunderstanding. Had the Pentedatelini thought fit to roll stones on the intruder, his fate must have been hard; but they seemed filled with fear alone. I left this wonderful place with no little regret, and rejoining Ciccio, a soon lost sight of Pentedatilo, pursuing my way up the stream."[2]

Clearly, Lear's literary description of the mountain with its emphasis on the magical, the wild, the savage, awe of its vastness and height, and the brooding darkness and terror of the place are Sublime in content. His painterly transcription breathes emotional life into the landscape. The contrasts of light and dark, the rich, painterly build-up, the vertical format, impress the viewer with the immediacy of the place and a sense of being surrounded by its scale and mystery. Further following the Burkian formula regarding the Sublime, the emotional impact of the painted landscape is due to obscurity and contrast within the elements of the picture; subdued coloration with emphasis on browns, blacks, purples; a sense of vastness and of the infinite and timeless.

The technical formulas which constituted Picturesque landscape painting such as qualities of roughness, contrast and irregularity, could also be put to use in more pastoral and less grandiose subjects. This quietist version of the Picturesque was well described in essays

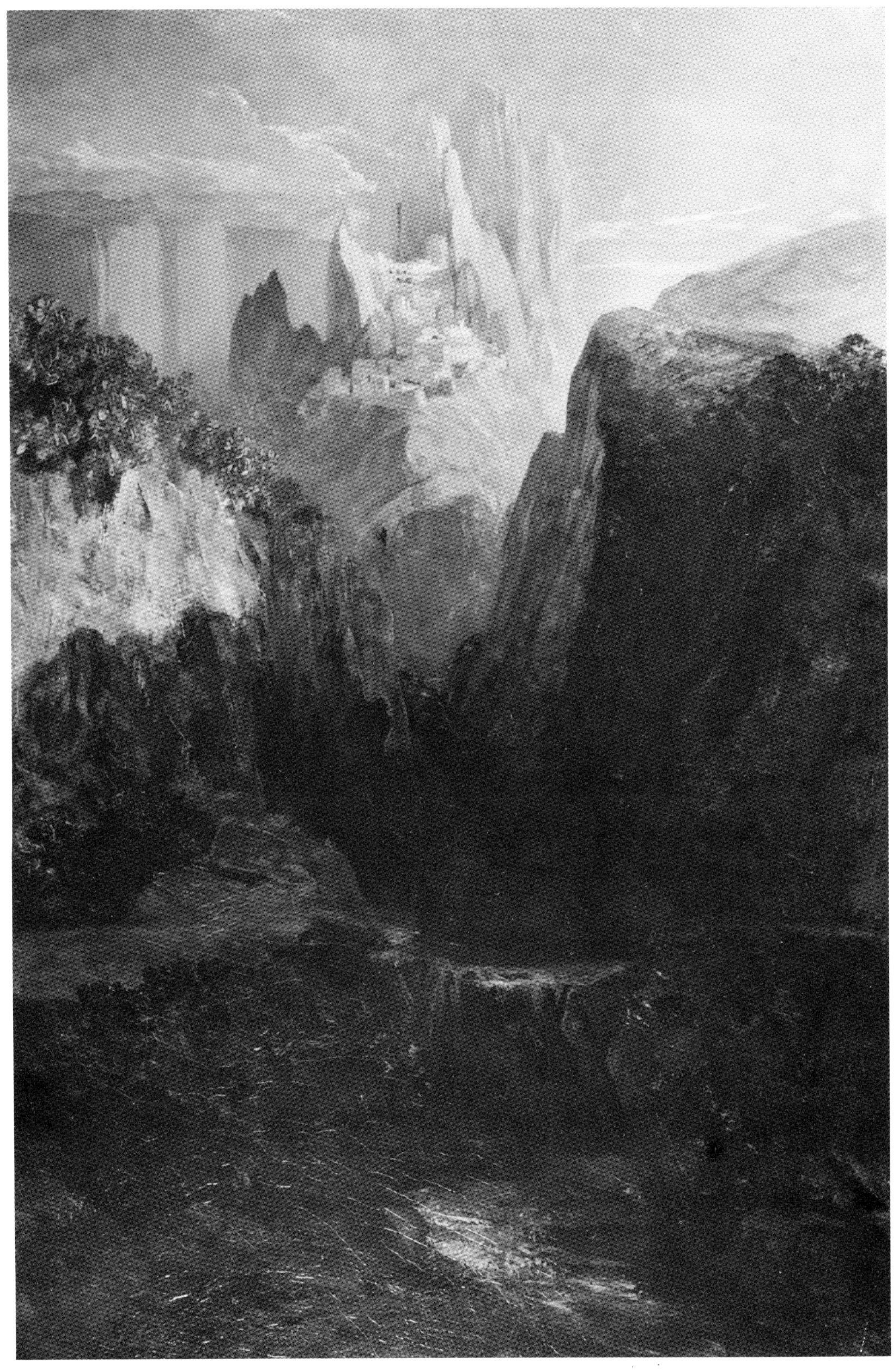

Fig. 2 Edward Lear (1812–1868)
    Pentedatilo. 1851
    Oil on canvas, 55 × 37″
    Museum Purchase
    1968.15

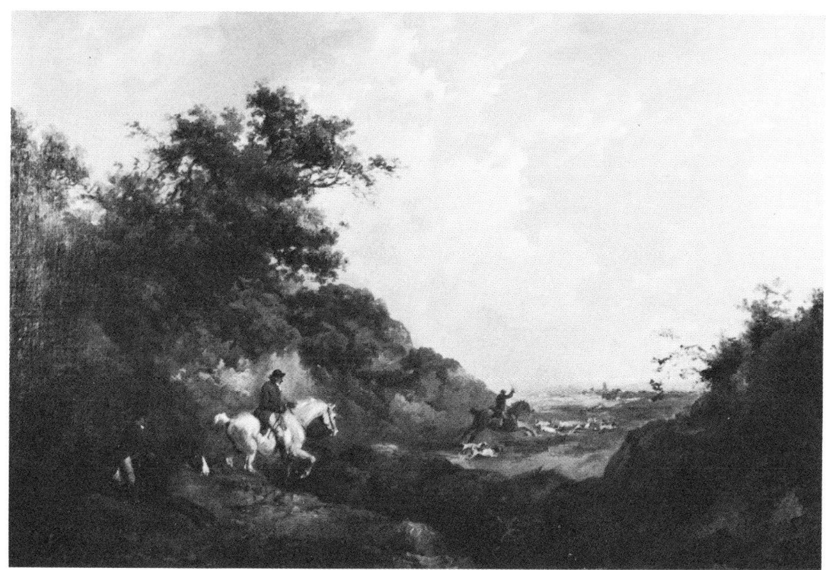

Fig. 3 George Morland (1763–1804)
 Landscape. 1798
 Oil on canvas, 19¼ × 25″
 Gift of the Children of Dwight W. and Elizabeth
 C. Morrow, '95
 1955.459

by Sir Uvedale Price (1794), the Rev. William Gilpin (1802) and Richard Payne Knight (1805), all of whom analyzed the observation of the *everyday* landscape. This quietist or pastoral interpretation of landscape was a middle ground between the vastness, terror and grandiosity of the Burkian Sublime and the calm gentleness of the Beautiful also described by Burke and to be discussed later.

George Morland's (1763–1804) *Landscape*, 1798, (fig. 3) shows this peculiarly English sense of the "cottage style" Picturesque. Morland, a child prodigy, was an amalgam of influences. He was influenced by the quietude of the Dutch landscapists Cuyp and Potter as well as the Rococco activity of the French eighteenth-century artists. Morland's hunt scenes, and his pictures of gypsies and banditti, refer to the active nature of Rococco painting and the activity of subject matter associated with the Sublime. But the plein-air realism of his approach to landscape serves as a precursor to the rise of Romantic landscape painting.

Three other practitioners of this quietist interpretation of Picturesque are represented in the collections at the Mead Art Museum. The first, John Linnell (1792–1882), was the leader of a group of landscape painters who made their headquarters at Linnell's home at Hampstead. The circle included the Varley brothers (Cornelius and John) and such visionaries as Samuel Palmer and William Blake. It was Linnell who encouraged Blake and commissioned from his friend the engravings for the *Book of Job* (see page 58). While Linnell's work is very different from Blake's, it is surely bathed with no less poetic sensibilities and contains a magical reverence for the emotions inspired by the most commonplace natural settings.

In Linnell's *Landscape* (fig. 4) the elements of the Picturesque are easily discerned. The irregularity of the landscape, the mellowed contrasts of light and shade, a sense of transience and moving light, asymmetry of composition all please the Picturesque eye. Of further significance is the amount of space and importance given over to the sky. No longer a dull appendage to a landscape picture, the drama of the sky is fully developed. It is such attention to moving, transient light and changing forms that inspired the cloud studies of John Constable during the 1820's.

In David Cox's (1783–1859) *Sussex Windmill* (fig. 5) the dramatic importance of the sky recalls the Netherlandish pictorial tradition of atmospheric, wind-swept and rain soaked fields and heaths. His responses to nature were as immediate as Constable's, and the surfaces of his pictures, rough and varied. Indeed he replied to criticism of his work saying, "these are works of the mind, which I consider very far before portraits and places."[3] Beyond the painterly contrasts and textures upon the surface of the canvas, both Linnell's and Cox's landscape paintings are filled with associative meanings also part of Picturesque taste.

These associative meanings of the landscape appeal to the viewer's internal rather than external sensibilities. As a mode of vision, rather than just a manner of seeing, the Picturesque was meant to touch upon what was eternal and basic to nature itself. As Price pointed out, the associations that the viewer made *in memory* with ruins, hovels, and fields, went beyond the external view of such things to perceptions or ideas that entered the realm of sentiment.[4] Linnell incorporates such external elements which are meant to produce internal associations. The observer cannot help but think of the vir-

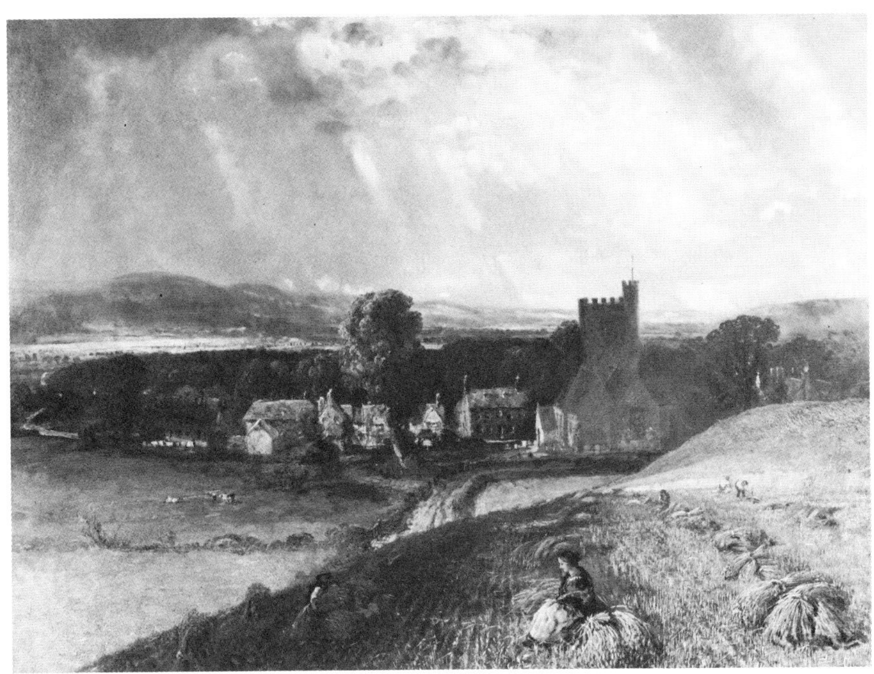

Fig. 4 John Linnell (1792–1882)
Landscape
Oil on Canvas, 19½ × 26½"
Gift of Calvin K. Arter
1960.110

tuousness and timelessness of the rural landscape, and of peasant life or work. The passage of time and its very continuity are further suggested by the village church— a reference to medieval times.

Interest in medievalism was an integral part of the cult of the Picturesque. Not only did ruins provide the necessary "visuals" for picturesque appreciation in their texture, irregularity, contrasts of light and dark, asymmetry—but they also contained associative meanings which evoked sentiment and memory. Further, medieval structures were to be found inextricably linked with English rural village life, as Linnell's painting shows. The interest in the Middle Ages also precipitated architects and connoisseurs to erect new ruins or castles in order to improve upon the past and create even better Picturesque associations. One such building was Fonthill Abbey (fig. 6), built for collector and connoisseur William Beckford by architect James Wyatt. Fonthill in 1796 was a favorite subject for artists such as Scotsman Robert Gibb (d. 1837), who were interested in the Picturesque. It incorporated all the required elements of the irregular and asymmetrical, and its dramatic profile against a churning sky all point to early Romanticism. The 230-foot octagonal central tower rising over a 120-foot-high great hall incorporated those elements of height, awe and astonishment so central to Burke's definition of the Sublime. Indeed, if the future could have been read, the terror associated with Sublimity might have been appropriate, for the structural

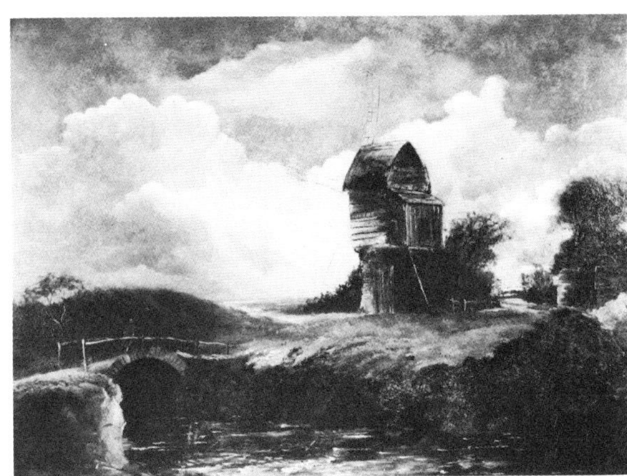

Fig. 5 David Cox (1783–1859)
A Sussex Windmill
Oil on board, 13¼ × 17¾"
Gift of Calvin K. Arter
1960.102

supports of Fonthill were inadequate and the great tower collapsed in 1825.[5]

Gibb's view of Fonthill was probably executed around 1823 and is very similar to John Martin's view of the same subject. John Martin (1789–1854), an immensely popular painter, apprenticed as a glass enameler and his mature work is marked by his early interest in opaque but vivid colors and a tight, smooth handling of paint. He was obsessed with scale and proportion,

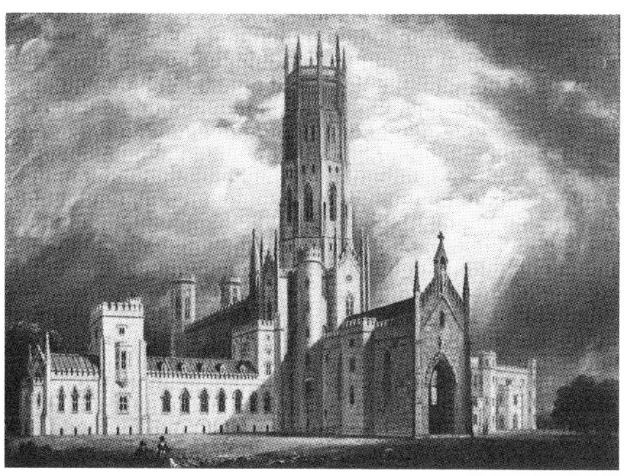

Fig. 6 Robert Gibb [The Elder] (1801–1837)
   Fonthill Abbey, 1826
   Oil on canvas, 11½ × 15¾″
   Museum Purchase
   1953.62

usually including very small figures in his expansive—often panoramic—landscapes. He usually chose literary subjects and set his stories in stretches of nature filled with towering rocky ledges or large architectural elements, giving height to the composition and contrast to the tiny figures. These characteristics associate his work with the attitudes of grandeur so important to the Sublime.

But Martin's picture, *Hermaphroditus and Salamacis*, 1814, (fig. 7) provides us an opportunity to explore the opposite but related issue of the Burkian Sublime—the Beautiful. According to Burke, Beauty is not dependent upon perfection or proportion, but the cause of Beauty is that which inspires Love. Some of those qualities Burke enumerated were dimunition which inspires tenderness, smoothness and polish of surfaces,

gradual variation, delicacy or a sense of fragility, colors which are clear, bright, but not strong or glaring. These qualities of Arcadian landscape painting are recognizable in Martin's *Hermaphroditus and Salamacis*. The overall smoothness and flowing delicacy of line are in marked contrast to the more rugged landscape of Linnell. Martin's landscape is composed and imaginary. It does not have the immediacy of the early nineteenth-century Picturesque emphasis on atmospheric, luminous effects in the imitative depiction of landscape. In Martin's landscape, reverie is evoked by the introduction

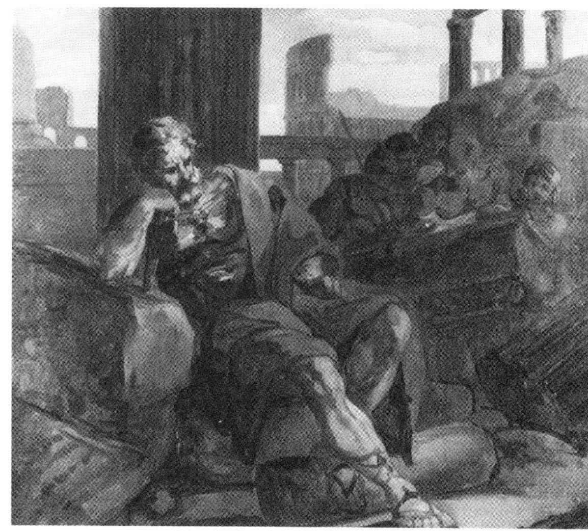

Fig. 8 Thomas Barker of Bath (1769–1847)
   Marius, ca. 1790–93
   Oil on paper, laid on canvas, 20 × 18″
   Museum Purchase
   1984.15

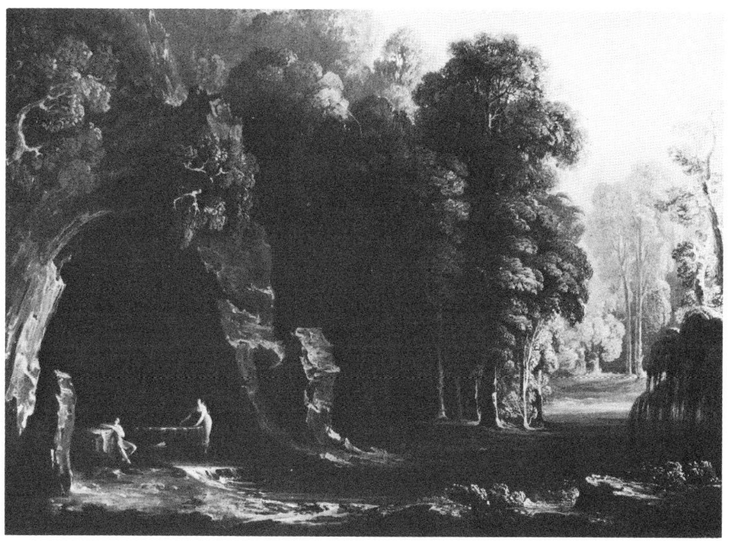

Fig. 7 John Martin (1789–1854)
   Salamacis and Hermaphroditis, ca. 1814
   Oil on canvas, 17 × 23½″
   Museum Purchase
   1976.67

of the languorous classical figures, the gentle flowing pool, the graceful willow tree and the pleasant associations of mythology. The son of Mercury and Venus, Hermaphroditus was pursued by the water nymph Salamacis. His rejection of her advances only spurred her efforts. Coming upon Hermaphroditus bathing in the pool, she held him so tightly that their bodies fused and formed one body—now both male and female.

Those qualities defined by Burke or Price or others as essential to the Picturesque, the Sublime or the Beautiful became less distinct categories. With the blurring of these distinctions came full-blown Romanticism. In *Marius Amid the Ruins of Carthage*, ca. 1790–93 by Thomas Barker of Bath (1769–1847), (fig. 8) one sees this synthesis in an early Romantic painting. Barker painted this picture while a student at the French Academy in Rome. It retains a classical subject, so popular in eighteenth-century Italian and French painting. Marius is seated in a languid, classical pose among Picturesque ruins. These once beautiful ruins are Picturesque not

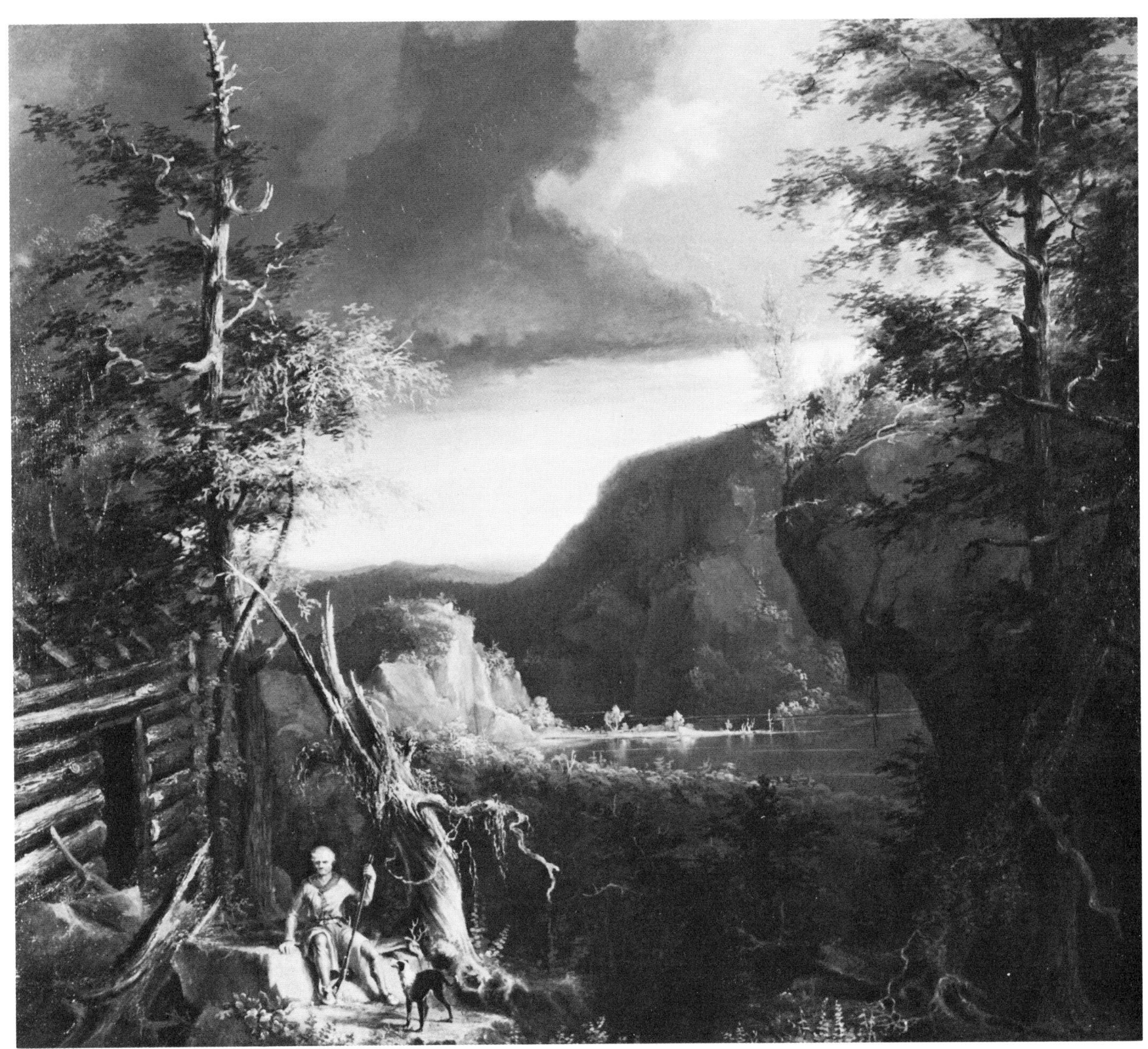

Fig. 9 Thomas Cole (1801–1848)
Daniel Boone and His Cabin on the Great Osage Lake,
ca. 1825/26
Oil on canvas, 38 × 42½″
Museum Purchase
P1939.7

only in their rugged textural quality, but also for their associative value with ancient civilization, the rise and fall of men's fortunes, and the passage of time. Further, these architectural elements point to the awe the viewer feels at the power of that civilization and the Sublime passions aroused by its collapse. The dark, gloomy atmosphere further lends itself to the fearful feelings inspired by the Sublime.

The desolation of a culture, a city, a landscape is complete, and Marius, contemplating death and destruction, matches this desolation in his mood. His is a figure no longer neoclassically Beautiful, not quaintly Picturesque, nor overcome with awe. In the fusion of mood and landscape he is a Romantic symbol. Barker's picture serves as an important image in a trans-atlantic sense also. The figure of Marius is akin to that of Daniel Boone seated in front of his cabin, also in the collection of the Mead Art Museum (fig. 9). The same overlay of Classical and Romantic imagery which permeated British art of the late eighteenth and early nineteenth centuries affected an entire generation of American painters who traveled and studied abroad, and who fused the character of the American wilderness with Romantic mood.

FOOTNOTES

1. Edmund Burke, *A Philosophical Inquiry into the Origin of Our Ideas of the Sublime and Beautiful,* Section II, Part II, ed. J.T. Baulton (London: Routledge & Paul, 1958).

2. Edward Lear, quoted in Peter Quennell, *Edward Lear in Italy: Journals of a Landscape Painter in Southern Calabria and the Kingdom of Naples,* (London: B.W. Kimber, 1964), pp. 151–53.

3. Trenchard Cox, *David Cox,* (London: Phoenix House, 1947), p. 105.

4. Christopher Hussey, *The Picturesque; Studies in a Point of View,* (New York: G.P. Putnam's Sons, 1927), pp. 79–81.

5. T. S. R. Boase, *English Art, 1800–1870,* (Oxford: Clarendon Press, 1959), pp. 25–28.

BRITISH WATERCOLORS
by Frank Trapp

The appeal of watercolor was long recognized by artists of many lands, but it was in eighteenth-century Britain that the medium gained an unprecedented popularity within the evolution of European art. To be sure, such major masters as Dürer found watercolor techniques advantageous for making records of their travels or accumulating visual documentations which could be easily stored for future reference. Nor was the practicality of an aqueous medium as a quick-drying vehicle for rendering all manner of image, whether in the most summary and fleeting of suggestion or in painstaking detail, lost on artists, once the supply of suitable papers and pigments became available to them. However, renditions in watercolor were traditionally regarded as ancillary products, hence more as a branch of drawing than as independent creations. Hence, while the toned drawings produced in some number by such artists as Adrian van Ostade (1610–1685) were, to be sure, sold as works of art in their own right, and admired accordingly, they were not the mainstay of their makers' livelihood or reputation. The emergence of watercolor as the medium of specialists, valued for its own qualities and standards of expression was a notable British contribution, as native artists began to build upon the foundations laid by foreign artists, mainly imported from the Low Countries during the seventeenth century. Two fine examples of works in the College collection which nicely illustrate the skills of such Netherlandish artists afford insights into the richness of the early watercolor tradition (Figs. 1 and 2). And, while the collection at Amherst College does not yet boast representation of the greatest British practitioners in that medium—no Turner, Bonington, or Constable—it does offer a variety of examples by note-worthy artists in which the evolution of its applications over the years may be appreciated.

Clearly, the larger cultural and artistic situation of the time had to be favorably disposed toward a development of the sort—as it was in many ways throughout western Europe. Without undue trust in positivist explanations, one may, for example, advance the proposal that in England, the foundation of the Royal Academy and the rise of an amateur constituency coalesced to foster developments of the sort. Though elitist in its assumptions of propriety and hierarchies of rank within the arts, the Academy was also a public-spirited organization devoted to the mission of teaching and service to the common good. In that sense, it was rather more democratically inclined than, let us say, its senior counterpart, the Royal Academy of France. And while the actual social structure of neither nation was yet "open" in the more modern sense, the intrusions of the bourgeosie upon aristocratic assumptions in cultural matters had progressed farther in England, where the feudal conventions had never had been so focally orchestrated as in the mature stages of the French monarchy. The desire of Sir Joshua Reynolds and his colleagues in founding the Royal Academy had been to ratify the stature of the fine arts as an intellectual pursuit, following earlier efforts to break away from the time-honored traditions of the guilds.[1] Curiously, their invitation of amateur interest and support for their own aspirations contributed to a climate of artistic involvement in which (as is now the case in many parts) the visual arts along with music and the dance were, so to speak, domesticated. At the same time, however, the Academy's insistence upon formal performance in oil painting cast watercolor into a dis-

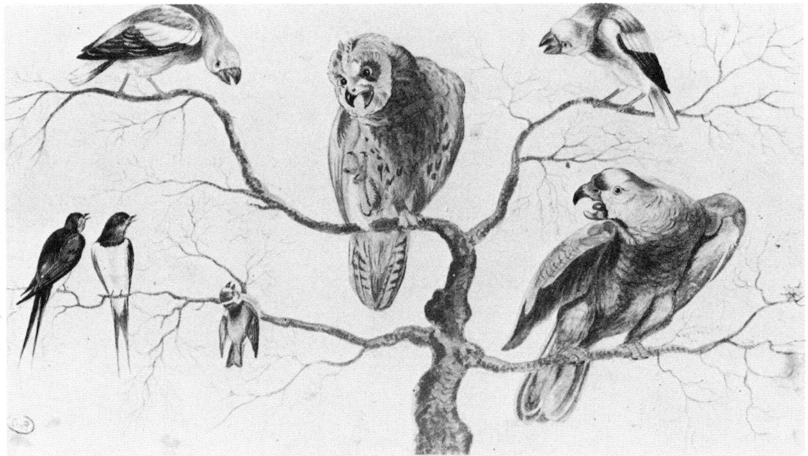

Fig. 1 Attributed to Jan Van Kessel (1626–1679)
Birds
Watercolor, 7 × 12″
Museum Purchase
1976.14

tinctly minor role, so that those who specialized in that cadet branch of representation finally instituted their own, independent societies. In doing so, they set a pattern of aspirations to professional autonomy which would long persist in the English-speaking world, within which nagging "ambiguities" of status and artistic purpose nevertheless persisted.[2]

For the practitioner, whatever his predispositions, watercolor had (and still retains) the great virtues of economy. Most often utilized for works comparatively small in scale, the materials were light and portable, so that conditions of execution were flexible: elaborate studio provisions were unnecessary and the option of working under informal conditions, whether indoors or out-

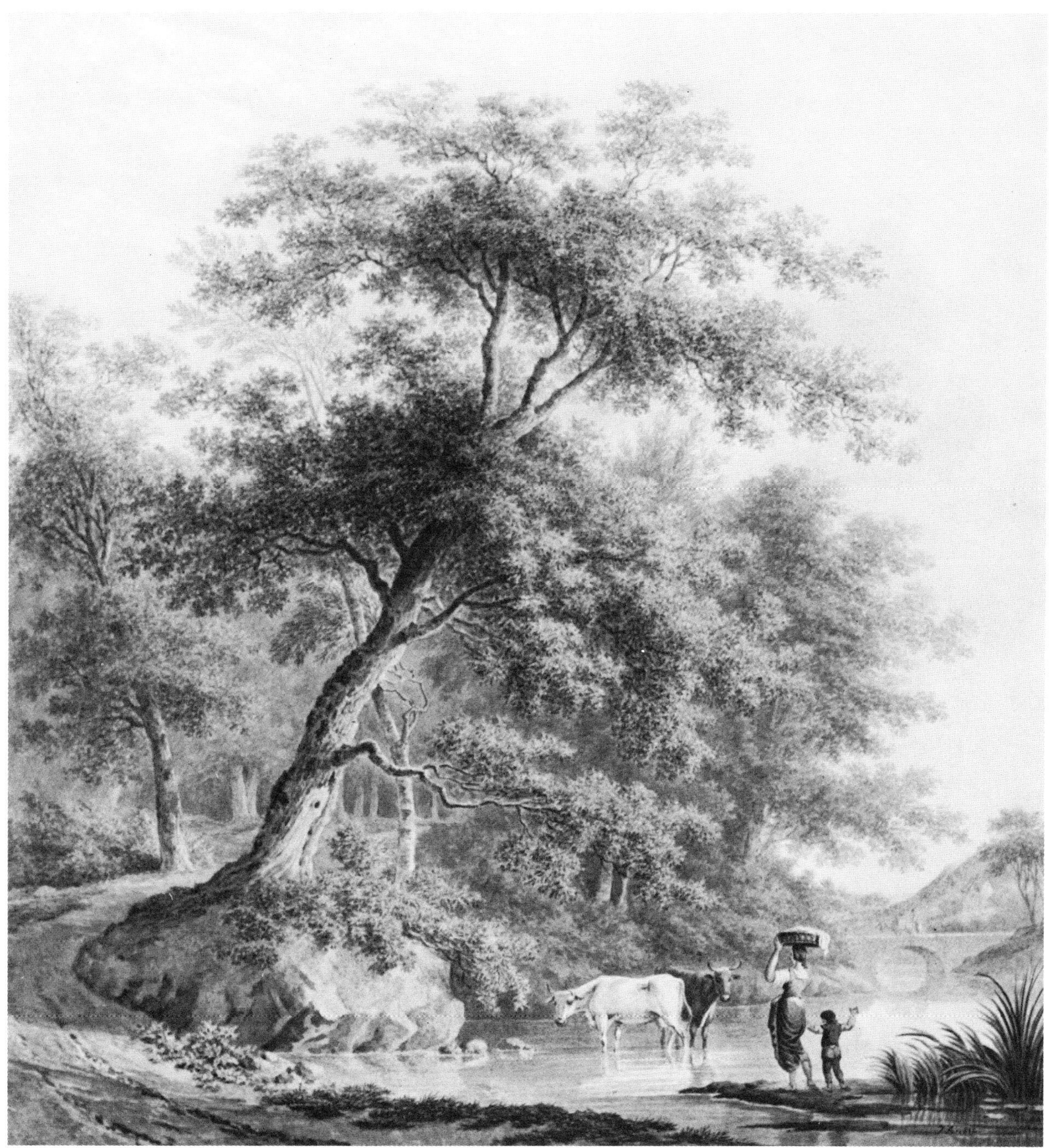

Fig. 2 Juriaan Andriessen (1742–1819)
Landscape with Figures and Cows By a Pond, 1812
Watercolor, Drawing 16⅝ × 17½"
Museum Purchase
1984.1

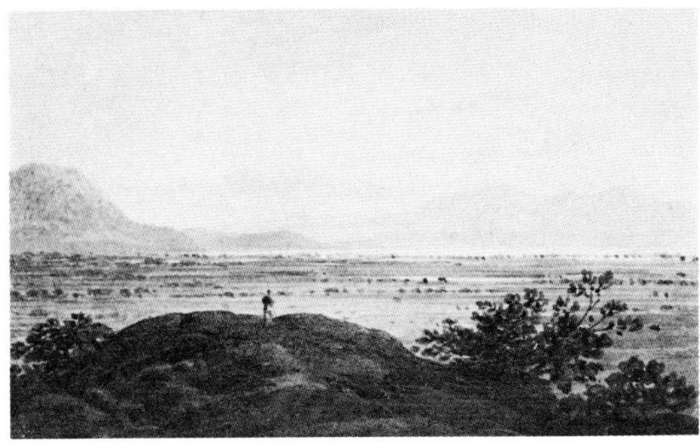

Fig. 3 John Varley (1778–1842)
The Plains of Marathon
Watercolor, 5 × 7¼″
Museum Purchase with funds from the
William K. Allison, '20 Memorial Fund
1985.22

of-doors, was invited. A new ease of working directly from the subject *en-plein-aire* eventually had significant implications, conceptually as well as materially. At another level, the young aspirant was freed from the traditional need for lengthy apprenticeship in the technically more complex formal mediums.

While special skills were, to be sure, required of the watercolorist, they were not necessarily coupled with the full repertory of accomplishments normally expected of a "professional" artist, for whom oil painting or the graphic processes, particularly engraving, would commonly serve as the cornerstone of reputation. Thus it was that many amateurs were in due course attracted to the practice of watercolor painting—often with some distinction—even as the drawing master came to play a role in the education of well brought-up persons. And

while British gentlewomen were surprisingly scarce in the initial ranks of watercolorists, by the latter part of the century they, too, were attracted to this form of cultivation in greater numbers.[3] In the early phases of this development, representational skills essential to that art were welcome among the swelling ranks of the Crown's military and naval officers or of civil servants in their promotion of the course of Empire. Well before the advent of the camera—and long after—watercolor images satisfied practical as well as vicarious fascinations of the age.

For the collector, watercolors held the great attraction of being intimate, informal, and often graced with the special qualities of freshness the medium invites. Being small and easily handled as well as less costly than oils, they came to be favored by a clientele which included connoisseurs of highly cultivated tastes. Some, such as the well known Dr. Thomas Monroe, enjoyed some training and skill as watercolorists in their own right—experiences which only whetted their enterprise as collectors. Indeed, "the good doctor's" activities as a dilettante extended well beyond his patronage of such favorite artists as Thomas Girtin, Joseph Mallord William Turner, and John Varley. His now famous "academy" at his London residence, No. 8 Adelphi Terrace, was a seed bed for young talent, where master examples could be studied and copied.[4] Thanks to enthusiasms of the sort, watercolorists came to be "as plentiful as blackberries" during the early years of the past century,[5] with their own societies devoted to the interests of their favored medium.

The body of works at Mead which illustrate the emergence of this characteristic tradition of English art and the broad lines of its development remains small but

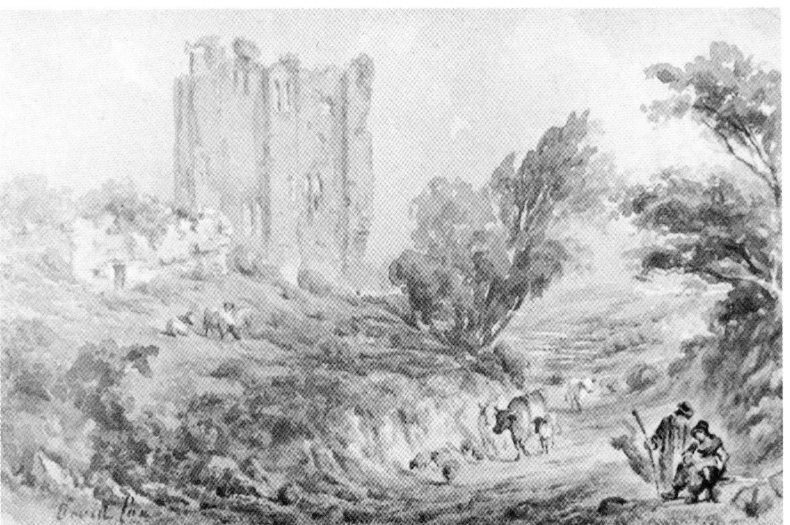

Fig. 4 David Cox (1808–1885)
The Castle
Watercolor, 7¼ × 11¼″
Gift of the Children of Elizabeth and
Dwight W. Morrow, '95
1955.463

42

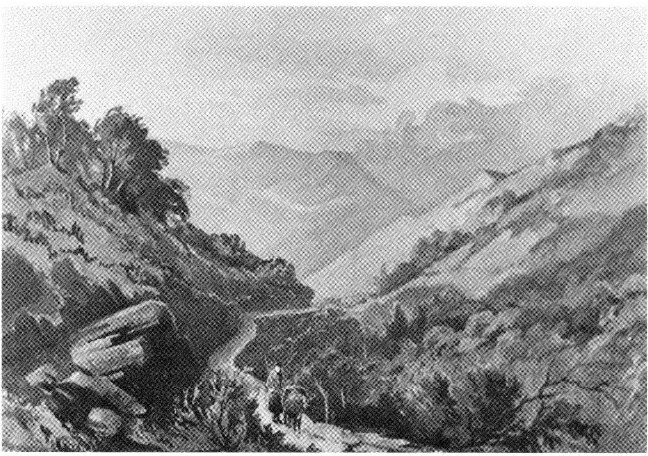

Fig. 5 Anthony Van Dyke Copley Fielding (1787–1855)
Landscape and Figures—Ireland. 1811
Watercolor, 6½ × 9½"
Gift of Professor Arthur H. Baxter
PWC 1937.10

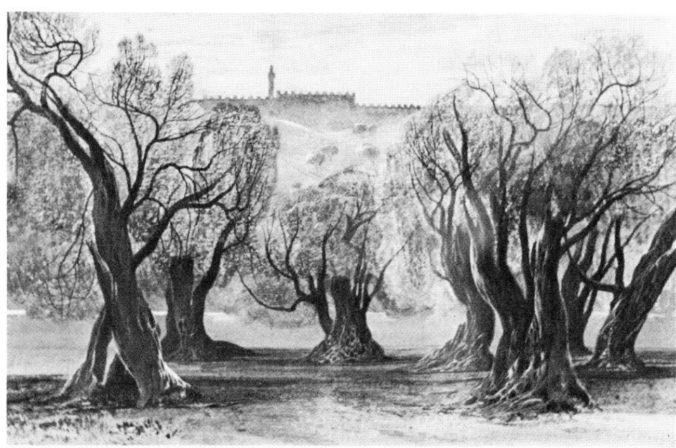

Fig. 6 Edward Lear (1812–1888)
Olive Trees in the Garden of Gethsemane
Watercolor, 6½ × 10¼"
Museum Purchase
1961.138

is fairly ample in range and high in artistic quality. An annotated review of the best and most characteristic of their number follows. It may be hoped that in due course this selection will be expanded to include further representations of that significant episode in the development of the British School of Painting.

JOHN VARLEY (1778–1842)

One of the most prolific early advocates of the watercolor medium and a protagonist of the Water-Colour Society, John Varley gained visibility as a protegé of Dr. Monro's and in turn, he himself came to enjoy the role of teacher. Varley's many pupils included John Linnell, Samuel Palmer, David Cox, Copley Fielding, and William Holman Hunt. Also given to mysticism, Varley remained a close friend of William Blake's from the time of their meeting in 1819, until the latter's death in 1827. During a long career he evolved a succession of manners. The small view of *The Plains of Marathon* (fig. 3), recently acquired for the Amherst College Collection, relates to his later manner. Though sometimes criticized as repetitious in their handling and less direct in spirit, Varley's works of these years are nevertheless often distinguished as here, by a romantic richness of atmospheric mood and an attractive resonance of subtly nuanced color. Since Varley never visited Greece, it may be assumed that this "view" derived from some intermediate topographic source of the kind he seems to have consulted more and more as an alternative to natural fact in his search for sources of thematic inspiration.

DAVID COX (1783–1859)

The influences of Salvator Rosa and Claude Lorrain were especially important to Cox as he turned to the rugged features of the Welsh highlands. In his use of the watercolor medium he was also indebted to the techniques employed by John Varley, with whom he studied for a time and whose example he followed in exploring the beauties of the Welsh countryside. During his middle and late years, Cox was especially attracted to subjects drawn from North Wales, centering on Bettws-y-Coed. In them he indulged his increasing confidence in a bold, fresh manner, in which his eventual fondness for the effects afforded by the use of rough-textured papers, as may be seen in the example illustrated (fig. 4), one of the two watercolors by his hand now in the Collection. Cox is also represented at Mead by a lively landscape in oils, in which his spontaneity may be admired.

THOMAS MILES RICHARDSON (1813–1890)

A regular participant in exhibitions held at the Royal Academy and elsewhere, Richardson came to be known for his production of agreeable landscape sketches of mountains and moors seen under cloud-filled skies. Grazing cattle sometimes provide enlivening, local notes. Richardson's technique is apt to be conservative compared to the more spontaneous modes of handling which increasingly came into fashion. His relatively close observation of natural detail, characteristically rendered in carefully reworked tones of color, was often touched with admixtures of opaque white. This side of Richardson's practice is especially evident in an *Italian Lake Scene* (fig. 7), one of two landscapes by Richardson in the Collection, both part of a gift of several British watercolors made by Professor Arthur H. Baxter in 1937.

ANTHONY VAN DYKE COPLEY FIELDING (1787–1855)

Another student of Varley's and the best known of a family of minor but capable artists, Copley Fielding was a productive and widely recognized specialist in watercolor painting. He and his brother Thales (also a watercolorist) were among Eugène Delacroix's favorite companions during his prolonged visit to London in 1825, and it was largely through the Fieldings that Delacroix learned to employ the novel "English" watercolor tech-

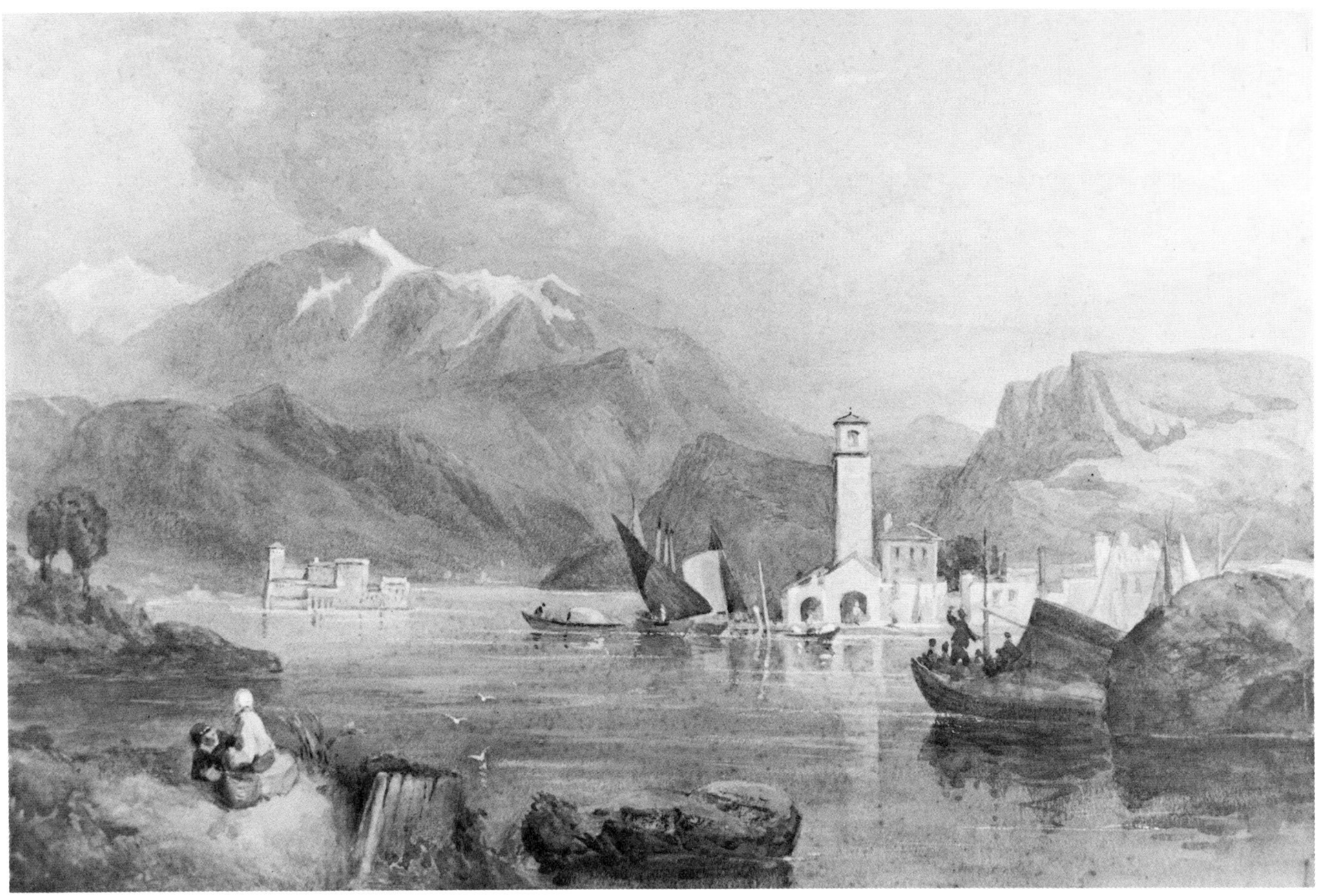

Fig. 7 Thomas Miles Richardson (1813–1890)
Italian Lake Scene. 1870
Watercolor on paper, 13 × 19¾"
Gift of Professor Arthur H. Baxter
PWC 1937.9

niques which were to gain widespread favor on the Continent. The brilliant but short-lived Richard Parkes Bonington (1802–1828) was another member of that congenial circle. Copley Fielding's own, not inconsiderable accomplishments as a watercolorist may be appreciated in the two attractive examples of his art in the Collection at the Mead Art Museum (fig. 5).

EDWARD LEAR (1812–1888)

Now more famous as the great master of nonsense verse, Lear sustained a lifelong career as a professional artist.[6] From age 15 he gained his livelihood making the colored drawings for use in the zoological publications, mainly those devoted to the study of birds. With his eyesight, impaired by the strain of those minute tasks, he eventually turned to the less exacting genre of landscape representation, and though physically frail in health, to periods of ambitious foreign travel. His wanderlust took him through the Balkans, the Holy Land, Egypt and North Africa, and then eventually, in 1872, to India and Ceylon. His annotated drawings in pen and ink as well as his more finished watercolor paintings resulting from those perigrinations are remarkable for their accurate yet spontaneous handling. Yet they are equally distinguished by a fine, often quite delicately nuanced sense of mood and place, as may be seen in the example at hand (fig. 6), with its novel coloristic resonances invited by the extended palette and new pigments of the day.

HERCULES BRABAZON (1821–1906)

Though a prolific and gifted watercolorist, Brabazon was at the same time an example of the British tradition of accomplished amateurism and love of travel. Following his formal education at Harrow, then at Trinity College, Cambridge, he turned to the serious study of watercolor, which he learned largely through copying earlier masters of that medium, including Cox. He soon came to be an ardent admirer of Ruskin's drawings and of Turner's developed manner. Overtones of the latter source of inspiration in particular are evident in Brabazon's fully characteristic works, which are broadly fluid and spontaneous in quality. Accomplished though he was, and voluminously productive, Brabazon rarely showed his work and was reluctant to sell. Blessed with the means to do so, he indulged his love of travel—a predilection vividly recalled in his many vibrant sketches of locales in Europe and Egypt. Brabazon's affection for skillfully manipulated washes of "body color" is often recalled in watercolors of John Singer Sargent, who greatly admired the older man's work and was visibly affected by it. The Venetian scene illustrated (fig. 8) is one of two subjects by Brabazon given to the College by Mrs. C. N. Bliss in 1949.

ROGER ELIOT FRY (1866–1934)

To some extent heir to longstanding British traditions of travel and artistic accomplishment as proper pursuits of the well bred, Fry turned to the serious study of painting following his own student years at Cambridge. While his posthumous reputation, like Lear's, came to rest mainly with his literary contribution, where he stands with his fellow artist Ruskin as a leading figure in art criticism, Fry was a gifted and devoted painter. The finely cultivated sensibilities which inform the artistic products of his hand corroborate the qualities of mind and spirit which inspired his performance as a critic. They may here be seen in a firmly constructed and expertly handled study, recently purchased for the Collection (fig. 9). In it, the traditional English employment of washes of translucent or opaque "body color" may be observed.

EDMUND BLAMPIED (1886–1966)

The last figure to be singled out in this synopsis, Blampied represents the no less honorable tradition of a more single-minded involvement in his craft, wherein he earned a wide following for his skillful performances, both as a painter and as a graphic artist. Blampied's much admired and copious production as an etcher and

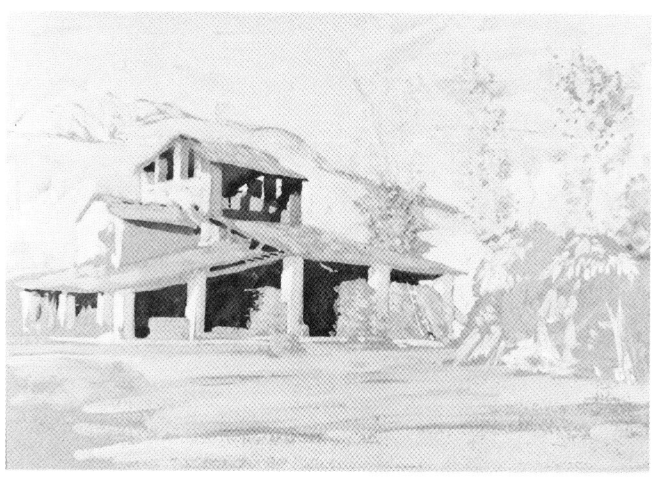

Fig. 9 Roger Fry (1866–1934)
The Brickfield in Italy
Watercolor, 13 × 9½"
Museum Purchase
1985.5

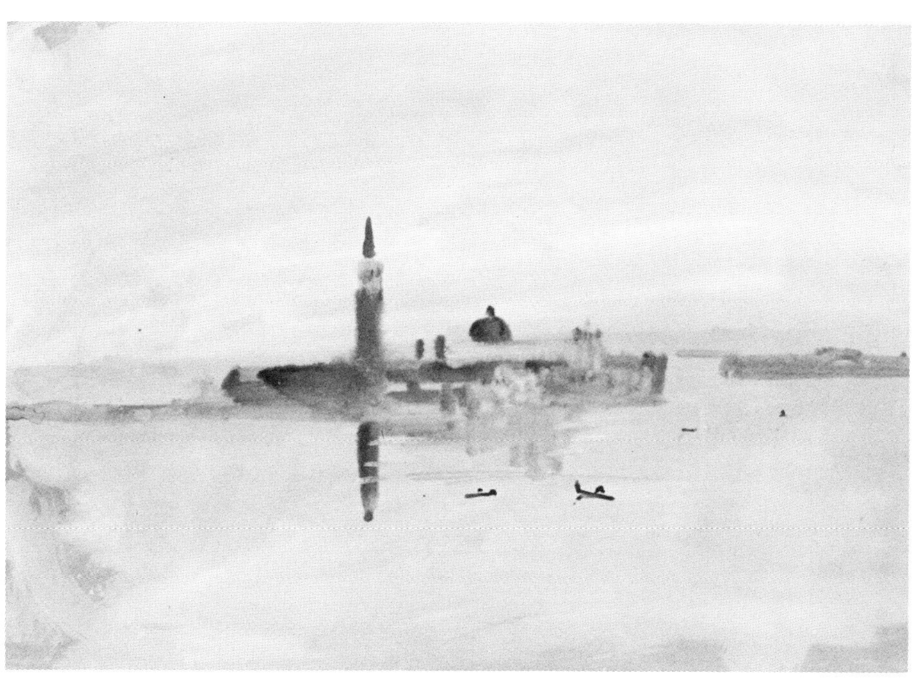

Fig. 8 Hercules Brabazon (1821–1906)
Murano
Watercolor, 9¾ × 13"
Gift of Mrs. C. N. Bliss
1949.28

lithographer is well represented in the Crossett Collection of prints, now part of the Mead Art Museum. His faculty for those techniques is echoed in the practiced freedom of his watercolors. In them, the well honed skills inherited from a long line of predecessors were put to the service of a clientele which admired his personal variations upon the established conventions of the watercolor medium (fig. 10).

There are other examples from the Mead Collection which might have been included in the present review, some of them of excellent quality. Among them, the spirited wash drawing, *The Money Changers*, by John Gilbert (1817–1897), may perhaps be better classed simply as a drawing. Certain other works such as a handsome *Portrait of a Lady*, 1833, by George Richardson (1809–1896) or another equally attractive female portrait of 1839 by Francis William Wilkins (ca. 1791–1842) are perhaps better considered as "Victoriana." The same may be said for studies by Ford-Madox Brown (1821–1893) and Edward Burne-Jones (1833–1898). Examples by American artists of the nineteenth century who worked extensively in Britain and in a comparable genre have been arbitrarily excluded as outside the limits of the present summary. However, their relationship to contemporaneous developments in Britain should at least be mentioned. Among them, Thomas Moran (1837–1926), John Singer Sargent (1856–1925) and James Abbott MacNeill Whistler (1834–1903) were especially noteworthy. All are represented by fine works of the kind in the Amherst College Collection, so that the interconnections between the kindred cultures which evolved in the two lands may be confirmed yet once again.

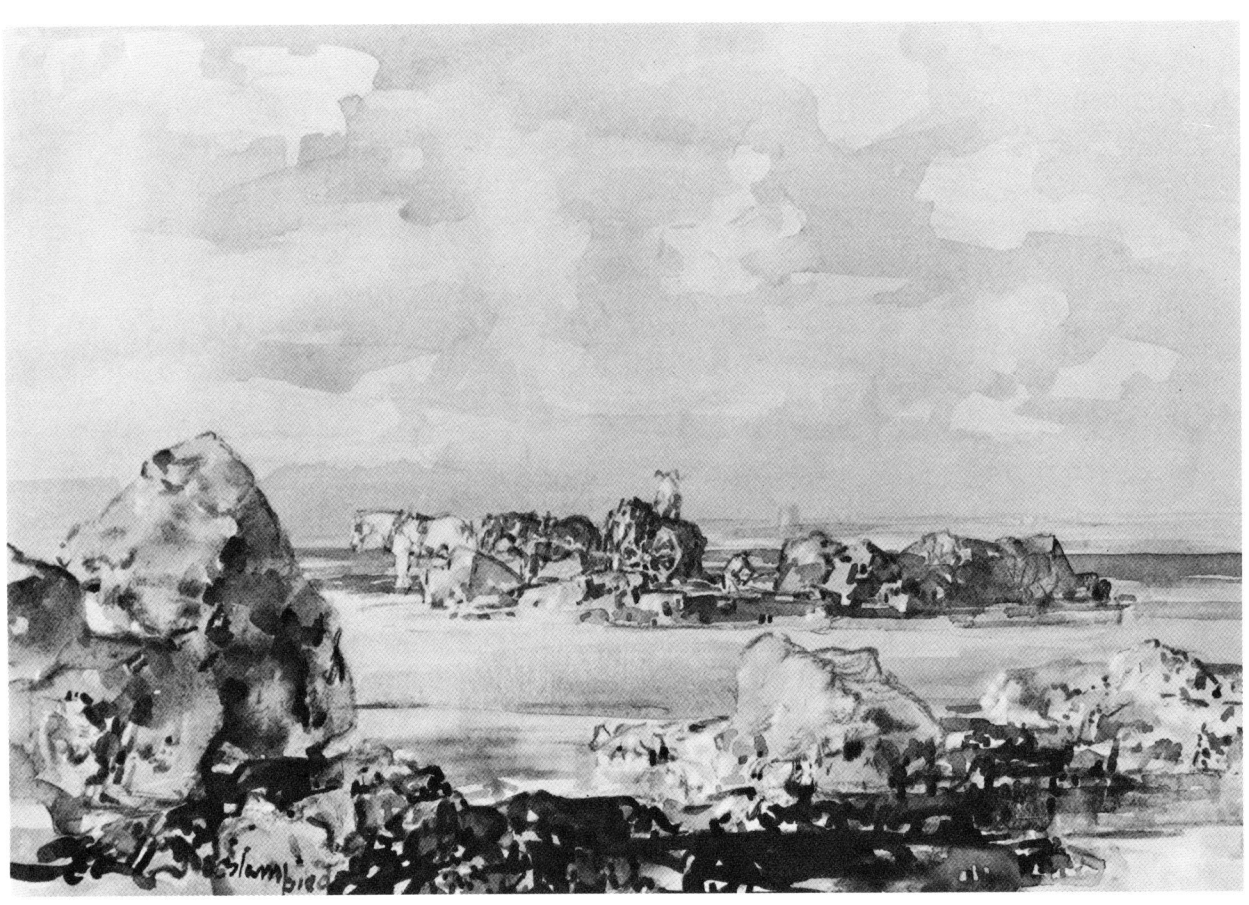

Fig. 10 Edmund Blampied (1866–1966)
Low Tide, Jersey
Watercolor, 13 × 18½"
Museum Purchase
1956.94

FOOTNOTES

1. The scholarly literature treating this important subject is both rich and extensive. An especially useful and comprehensive treatment of these complex developments is: Nikolaus Pevsner, *Academies of Art, Past and Present* (N.Y.: Da Capo Press, 1973), reprint of the 1940 ed. with new preface by the author. In more recent years many writers have usefully addressed this topic and its ramifications.

2. This question of identity has recently been discussed with particular reference to the Royal Society of Painters in Watercolors by Andrew Wilton. See, Andrew Wilton, "The Ambiguous Art of Watercolour," *The Antique Collector*, May 1985, Vol. 56, No. 5, pp. 80–85.

3. This rather surprising condition has been pointed out by Iolo A. Williams, *Early English Watercolours and Some Cognate Drawings by Artists Born Not Later Than 1785* (London: *The Connoisseur*, 1952), p. 248. In the fields of the so-called "applied arts," the situation was very different. Indeed, the very foundation of such institutions as the Victoria and Albert Museum was largely intended to provide suitable study models for the training of artisans, many of them women. The same patterns pertained to the coupling of museums and art schools elsewhere, not least of all in the United States.

4. For a sympathetic account of Monroe's contribution, see, Martin Hardie, *Water-Colour in Britain III, The Victorian Period* (London: B. T. Batsford, 1968), pp. 277–280.

5. Williams, *Op. Cit.*, p. 228.

6. The range of Lear's production as an artist has most recently been reviewed in a special exhibition of his works presented at the galleries of the Royal Academy, London, during the summer of 1985. See, Vivien Noakes, *Edward Lear*, (London: Royal Academy of Arts in association with Weidenfeld and Nicolson, 1985), 192 pages. Lear's large oil landscape, *Pentedatilo*, is discussed elsewhere in the present monograph.

ENGLISH REPRODUCTIVE PRINTS
by Christine Swenson

Amherst's remarkable collection of prints of all kinds offers a splendid source for investigating the art of reproductive printmaking, or the art of translating and communicating pictorial statements originally designed in another medium. Painters as their own printmakers or in collaboration with professional craftsmen have, throughout the history of graphic arts, worked to improve the capability of print media to transcribe as precisely as possible the character of paintings and drawings. Never, however, did the relationship between painters and the graphic arts produce more eloquent results than in England in the eighteenth and nineteenth centuries. As Amherst's collection reveals, the period from Hogarth to Landseer was the great age of the reproductive print.[1]

The era begins with William Hogarth (1697–1764), a painter with early training as an engraver. In the 1720's when Hogarth began his printmaking career, a copper-engraver in London had only two choices. He could sell his services outright to a printseller, of which there were fewer than twelve in London and Westminster, or he could struggle as an independent engraver with no way to distribute his prints. Hogarth combined his printmaking skills with entrepreneurship and became both engraver and publisher. He frequently etched and engraved the plates himself, to ensure the proper translation of his subject paintings, and he marketed his editions through subscription.

In 1732/33, capitalizing on his success with the six-plate set after his *Harlot's Progress* paintings, Hogarth engraved and published *Midnight Modern Conversation* (fig. 1) based on another painting.[2] The subject is a moralizing tale of the results of indulgence and the irony of the title is clear. The whole business of the evening is drinking, and all the stages, degrees and types of drunkeness are represented. Although the verse beneath the image begins, "Think not to find one meant Resemblance there / We lash the Vices but the persons spare," there is nevertheless a temptation to see characterizations of particular individuals. In fact, many of the revelers have been identified as friends and relatives of the artist as well as prominent politicians of the day.[3] *Mid-*

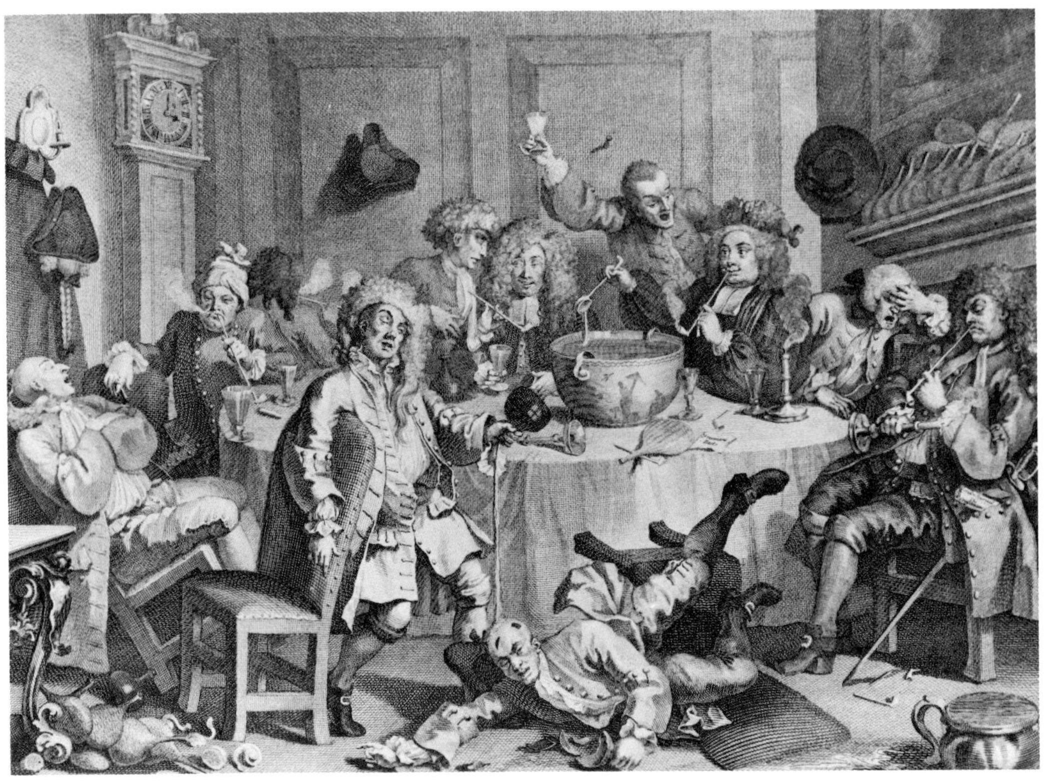

Fig. 1 William Hogarth (1697–1764)
A Midnight Modern Conversation, 1732–33
Engraving, 2nd state of 3, 13⅝ × 18½″
Museum Purchase with funds from the William K. Allison '20
Memorial Fund
1982.33

night Modern Conversation may very well be Hogarth's parody of the lively group portraits of Rembrandt and Hals or of the contemporary English conversation pieces, and it certainly shows his assimilation of the attitudes and conventions of the "low-life" genre in seventeenth-century Netherlandish painting.

There is another instructive inscription on the print: "Prints should be prizd (sic) as Authors should be read." Hogarth's paintings were visual equivalents of the literary work of his contemporaries, authors such as Jonathan Swift and Henry Fielding. He intended his prints to be read as narrative transcriptions of his paintings. Subordinating style to message, Hogarth chose the clarity of line etching and engraving to describe in detail the articles and events in his paintings. He used the freedom and speed of etching to lay in the basic composition and figures, then gained finesse and crispness of detail with the more precise technique of engraving. As a result, *Midnight Modern Conversation* has a sharpness of focus essential to the narrative. The painterly felicities and coloring of Hogarth's canvas may be absent, but the theatrical drama is clear. A simple documentary realism defines the scene in a regular system of lines. It is, in effect, Hogarth's equivalent of Swift's plain style, a straightforward presentation from which the horrible truths of human nature emerge.

Midnight Modern Conversation was enormously popular, as the numerous and remarkable variety of pirated versions and adaptations indicate. In addition to Hogarth's own, legitimate edition of this engraving, printsellers issued copies of the print and the image can also be found on everything from snuff boxs and punch bowls to fan-mounts.

This unbridled pirating of his prints (and his paintings) ceased only with the enactment of The Engravers' Copyright Act, which became law in 1735. Referred to as "Hogarth's Act," because of the artist's role in petitioning for the recognition of the value of an artist's work, this legislation is perhaps Hogarth's major contribution to print history. The law stipulated that the copyright of an artist's design remained legally protected for fourteen years. Under this act, Hogarth's paintings, his own engravings after these paintings, and his original prints were protected from pirated copies.

Marriage à la Mode, a set of six engravings issued in 1745 a few months after Hogarth had completed the

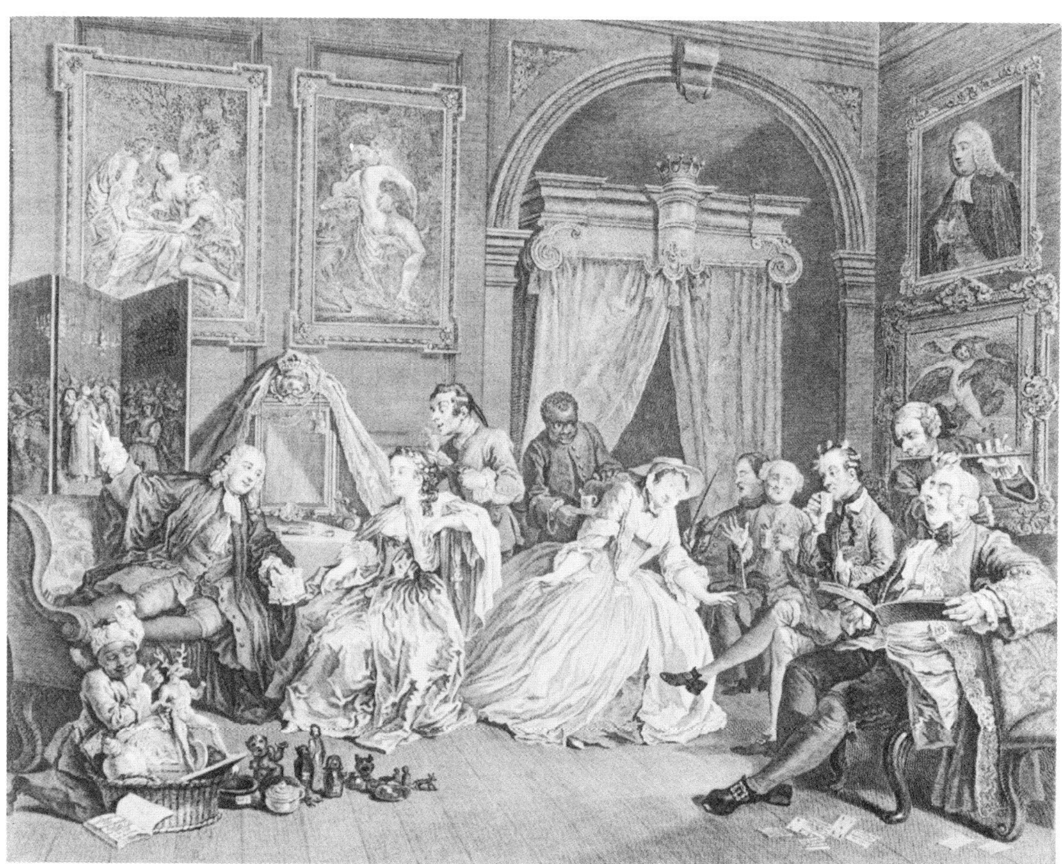

Fig. 2 Simon-François Ravenet (1710–1774)
 Marriage a la Mode, Plate IV: The Toilet Scene,
 1745
 Engraving, 15¼ × 18″, after William Hogarth (1697–1764)
 Museum Purchase
 1965.10d

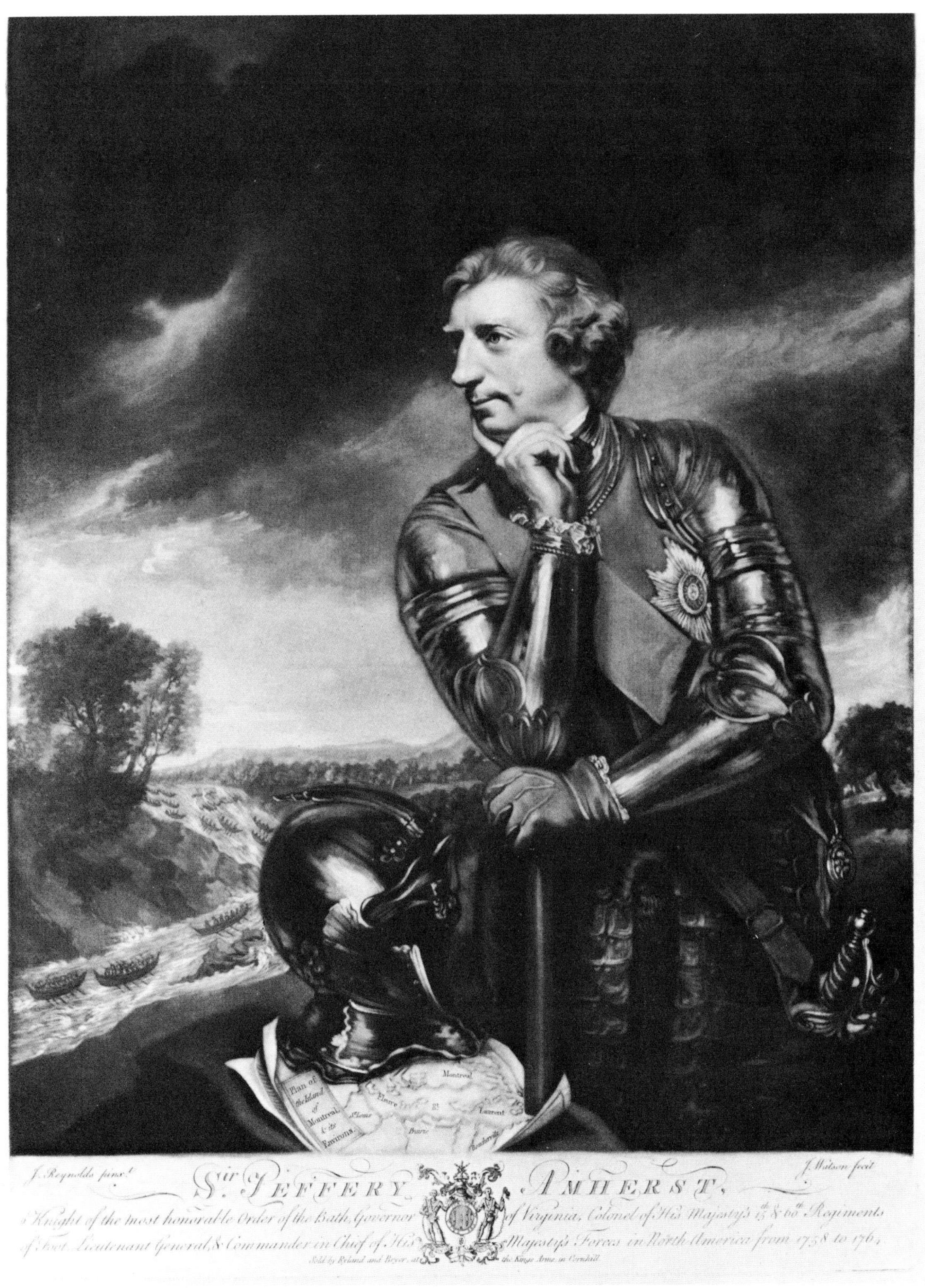

Fig. 3 James Watson (ab. 1739–1790)
Sir Jeffery Amherst
Engraving, 1766, after Sir Joshua Reynolds (1723–1792), 13 × 18½″
Gift of Dr. William J. Turner and Miss Isabel J. Turner
Pr 1939.90

paintings, was thus fully protected under the new law. The subject here was a conventional one of the day. Hogarth's story of the ill-matched merchant's daughter and Earl's son illustrates the argument that marriage can be based only on love, that disaster follows upon marriages arranged by parents and that marriage between a woman of money without class and a man of quality without money will end in unhappiness. In plate IV of the series (fig. 2) the young countess and her lover Silver-tongue, sit in a room peopled with characters and items that define and comment on the errant owner. This stage, the countess's boudoir, is hung with pictures of the "Loves of the Gods" and littered with bric-a-brac that includes Actaeon in horns and erotic drawings.

When planning his publications, Hogarth carefully considered what mode of engraving was best adapted to the translation of his paintings and to conveying his thematic intentions. Although he personally etched and engraved the plate for *Midnight Modern Conversation*, for *Marriage à la Mode* he employed the services of French engravers. The sophistication of their techniques provided a certain gracefulness of touch and Rococo elegance appropriate to the subject. Hogarth, however, reserved the engraving of the heads for himself, as would any self-respecting painter.

Hogarth, who may always be best known by prints, presented the English public with a form of moralizing and story telling familiar to the stage and novels but seldom seen in the visual arts. To those libraries that contained portfolios of portrait engravings and prints after Raphael and the Italian masters, the amateur could now add prints dealing with contemporary life and char-

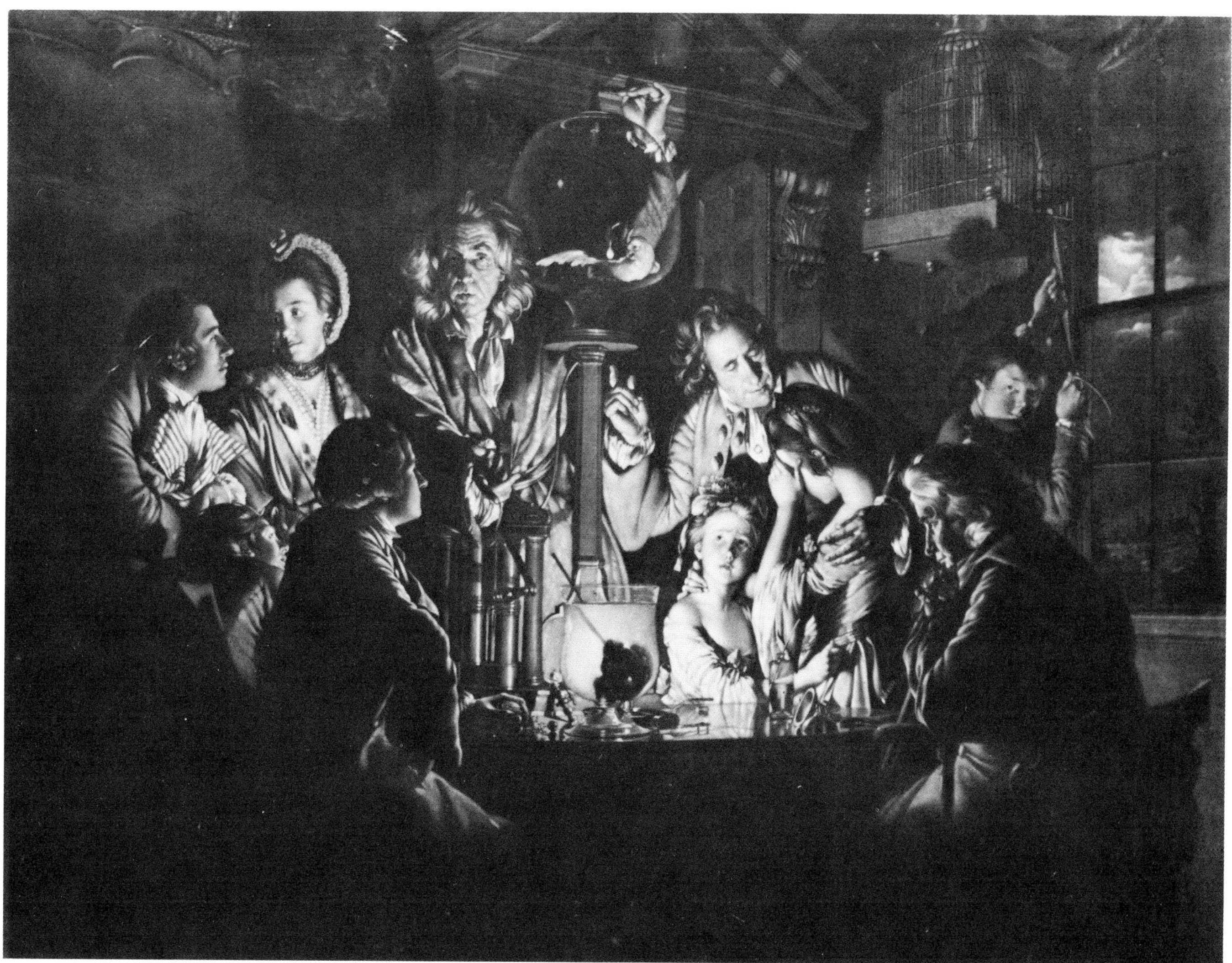

Fig. 4 Valentine Green (1739–1813)
A Philosopher Shewing an Experiment on the Air Pump,
1769
Mezzotint engraving, 17½ × 23″, after Joseph Wright
of Derby (1734–1797)
Museum Purchase
1950.28

acters in fictional form.

In prints as in paintings, however, portraits and not subject pieces dominated the market, if only in sheer numbers. The eminent clientele of British portrait painters clearly favored the publication of their likenesses. Sir Joshua Reynolds (1723–1792), one of the most fashionable portraitists in London in the 1770's and 1780's, was in fact the most engraved painter of the eighteenth century. His popularity as an artist depended as much on the engraved translations of his paintings as on the canvases themselves. He was astutely aware of the importance of engravings to his reputation and was particularly sensitive to the quality and finesse of the translations. He relied on the rich and suggestive tonal technique of mezzotint rather than the comparatively dry and descriptive technique of line engraving and etching for the reproduction of his richly surfaced canvases.

Mezzotint is a purely tonal technique, totally devoid of line. Unlike other print processes, mezzotint engraving works from dark to light. The entire surface of the plate is first abraded with a rocker, a multi-toothed tool which is literally "rocked" across the plate in every direction to pit the entire surface. If printed at this stage the plate would yield a solid and velvety black. To produce the image in tones from this deepest black to white, the engraver polishes the pitted plate by degrees with scrapers and burnishers, to flatten and re-smooth the surface. Mezzotint became the preferred process for interpreting paintings but particularly the portraits of the period, because of the medium's capacity to translate the rich effects of oil on canvas with a softness and subtlety

of effect. So popular and superbly used was this technique in England that it became known internationally as the "English manner" or "la manière anglaise."

Mezzotint achieved its first real success with Reynolds, who inspired his printmakers to achieve a new breadth of effect. The earliest transcriptions of his paintings were made in the 1740's by the Irish mezzotinter, James McArdell (ca. 1729–1765). McArdell led the group of Irish engravers who dominated mezzotint in mid-eighteenth-century London, infusing the medium with new standards of excellence.[5] After McArdell's early death, Reynolds turned to James Watson (1739–1790) and relied on this young Irish engraver's work for the next decade. Watson worked almost exlusively for Reynolds, and by the end of the 1770's he had done well enough in his profession to retire.

Sir Jeffery Amherst sat for Reynolds in May of 1765, shortly after returning from America, and the resulting portrait was exhibited the following spring. Watson's mezzotint after the painting (fig. 3) was issued simultaneously. The inscription declares Sir Jeffery's appointments, position and importance: "Sir Jeffery Amherst, Knight of the most honorable order of the Bath, Governor of Virginia, Colonel of His Majesty's 15th & 16th Regiments of Foot, Lieutenant General, & Commander in Chief of His Majesty's Forces in North America from 1758–1764." Watson's mezzotint captures the essence of Reynold's painting and simulates the appearance of paint on canvas, describing not only the distinguished likeness but brush strokes and layers of paint.

The Irish printmakers revitalized the technique and the market for mezzotints. The English engravers built

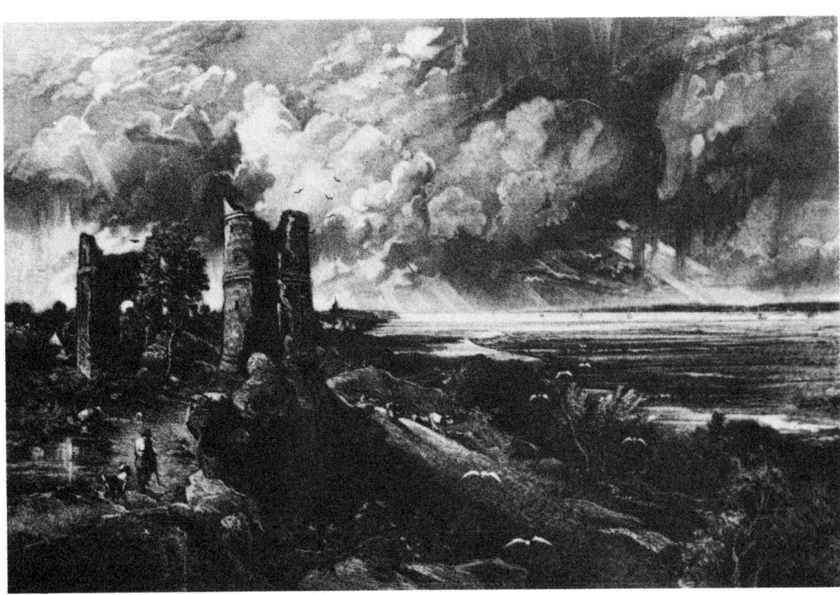

Fig. 5 David Lucas (1802–1881)
Hadleigh Castle Near the Nore
Mezzotint engraving, one of 22 in set, 1830–32,
10¼ × 14¼", after John Constable (1776–1837)
Museum Purchase with Funds provided by the Associates
of Fine Arts at Amherst
1979.4

on this foundation. They explored new themes and took the technique to new heights. Where the Irish had catered to the portrait market, the young English engravers such as Valentine Green (1739–1813), capitalized on the growing popularity of subject painting. The new factual view of the world led to fascinating new "fancy pieces," particularly the work of Joseph Wright of Derby (1734–1797). Green's mezzotints after the paintings of this pictorial prophet of the Industrial Revolution are some of the most outstanding images of the time. Wright's paintings with their dramatically lit stage sets were particularly well suited to spectacular translations into mezzotint. Green soon established himself as a master of the medium with such prints after Wright as *An Experiment on a Bird in the Air Pump* (fig. 4).[6] Published in 1769, a year after the painting was exhibited, the print was intended to provide the public with a substitute for the painting. It is large (17½ × 23 inches) and in the grand tradition of reproductive prints, was suitable for framing and hanging in the middle-class home.

The most painterly of all mezzotinters was David Lucas (1802–1881). A farmhand, Lucas learned printmaking at the age of 19, and in his 30's scraped some forty landscapes after paintings by John Constable (1776–1837). Painter and printmaker worked together on Constable's one, concerted attempt to use engravings to publicize his paintings. First published in 1830, the series of twenty-two mezzotints was re-issued in 1833 under the title, *Various Subjects of Landscape, Characteristic of English Scenery, Principally Intended to Mark the Phenomena of the Chiar'oscuro of Nature.*[7] Amherst

is fortunate to have this complete second edition, two of which are illustrated here (figs. 5, 6).

Constable was intimately involved in the working process. He repeatedly wrote to Lucas with instructions. Lucas in turn submitted as many as thirteen trial proofs per image to Constable, who would correct them with black lead and white paint until the impressions finally captured the reflections and sparkle of a country stream or the drama of light breaking through rain-filled clouds.

Lucas adapted the mezzotint process to achieve an effect appropriate to his subject. Rather than preparing the entire plate with a dark ground and then burnishing in the grays and whites, a technique that renders smooth tonal transitions and obscures the pattern of the rocker, Lucas started with a middle gray. He prepared the plate to the middle value and then worked up to white and down to black with burnisher and rocker. Thus Lucas kept his mezzotints on a higher key more in keeping with Constable's palette. The grays sparkle with dots of black and white, emulating the play of pigment on Constable's canvas.

These prints were not intended to be mounted on the wall as surrogates for the originals, but like J. M. W. Turner's *Liber Studiorum* (1807–1819), the prints were conceived as a collection of the artist's landscape designs. However, where Turner and his engravers presented a compendium of landscape types, Constable and Lucas published an essay on landscape, treating the specific conditions in particular localities, or, as the title indicates, the phenomenology of the English Countryside. Although Lucas proved to be a sympathetic interpreter of Constable's observations of Nature's tran-

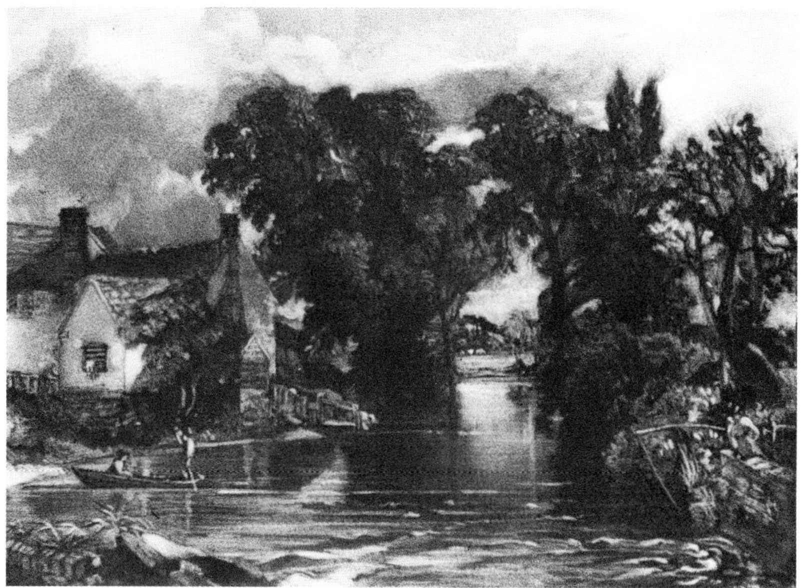

Fig. 6 David Lucas (1802–1881)
  Mill Stream
  Mezzotint engraving, one of set of 22, 1830–32,
  10¼ × 14¼", after John Constable (1776–1837)
  Museum Purchase with Funds provided by the Associates
  of Fine Arts at Amherst
  1979.4

science, the publication venture was a commercial failure.

Lithography, the first fundamentally new printing process invented since the fifteenth century, was developed in 1798 in Bavaria by Alois Senefelder and brought to England in 1801.[8] Senefelder's discovery was a method of printing based on chemical principles and the interaction of substances, not the variation of levels of surface. The technique is based on the natural aversion of water and grease and the affinity that limestone has for both. Marks made with a greasy chalk or ink on lithographic stone, preferably Bavarian limestone, accept the printer's ink, while the moistened stone does not, making it unnecessary to engrave or etch lines in the surface in order to prepare it for printing. With Senefelder's method the image was drawn on the surface and printed directly from the marks made.

Not until the English printer Charles Hullmandel set up his press in London in 1819, however, was there a sensitive and qualified printer totally devoted to artists' lithography. He worked closely with artists throughout the 1820's and 1830's to refine techniques that would be sympathetic to the draughtsman's intentions and methods. By the mid-1820's he had developed methods of handling chalk on stone that the artist could use to obtain consistent results and a wide range of tonal possibilities.

Cora, a Labrador Bitch (fig. 7) is the result of Hullmandel's collaboration with Sir Edwin Landseer (1802–1873), the celebrated Victorian painter whose subjects were eagerly sought by engravers and publishers.[9] Although Landseer generally engaged professional printmakers to engrave and lithograph his paintings, he had received early training in engraving and he did occasionally make his own plates. *Cora*, however, is one of his rare attempts to reproduce a painting in lithography. Drawing on the stone himself under Hullmandel's instruction, Landseer used cross-hatching of short parallel chalk marks laid closely together to develop luminous grays and strong blacks. These strokes of the lithographic chalk give the print the appearance of a drawing. Lithography at this stage in its development was essentially a drawing medium. Hullmandel did not perfect a wash technique that could suitably emulate paintings for another ten years. Landseer has, then, interpreted his painting as a printed drawing. The subject and composition of the painting are reproduced, but the physical properties of oil on canvas are not imitated.

Far more common than such autographic transcriptions by Landseer were the translations of his work by professional engravers. Reproductions of Landseer's paintings were made in a variety of media and range of

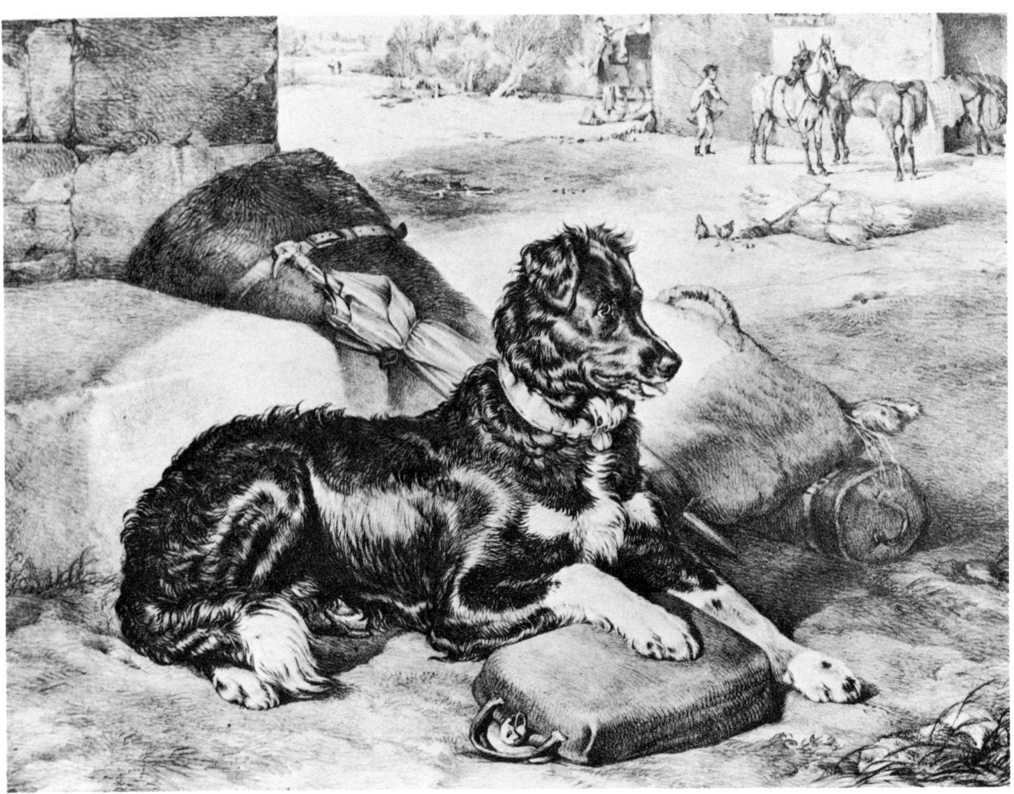

Fig. 7 Charles Joseph Hullmandel (1789–1850)
Cora, A Labrador Bitch, 1823
Lithograph, 14 × 17¼", after Sir Edwin Henry
Landseer (1802–1873)
Museum Purchase
Pr xx 80

sizes and editions. In 1874, a year after the painter's death, it was estimated that his interpreters numbered 126, and nearly 600 different printed versions of his subjects had been published. Like Constable, Landseer gave considerable attention to these reproductions of his work. He would touch proofs, give instructions and admonish his engravers to feel the subjects as he had, and to convey the sentiments of the picture not merely reproduce the image.

Charles George Lewis (1808–1880), a childhood neighbor and friend of the Landseer family, was one of Edwin Landseer's most prolific engravers. The portrait of the noble *Lion* (fig. 8) is only one of sixty plates Lewis engraved after Landseer's paintings. To meet the growing demands of Victorian print-publishing, Lewis chose to work in line-engraving. It was more durable than mezzotint and could more effectively simulate paintings than lithography. Lewis used a ruling machine to facilitate the production of the plate, eliminating a considerable amount of tedious hand work. The tool allowed Lewis to lay in parallel lines quickly and systematically for the broad general areas of sky and background. Like Hogarth a hundred years earlier, Lewis used a combination of etching and engraving, but the capabilities of the medium had advanced considerably and Lewis was able to take advantage of an increased flexibility and versatility.

Mezzotints, however, were still unsurpassed in the emulation of the painted surface. Samuel Cousins (1804–1887) who also engraved Landseer's work, was one of the most prestigious mezzotint engravers of the Victorian era. He used the technique with dazzling results, as for example in his print after Sir Thomas Lawrence's portrait of *Sir Robert Peel* (fig. 9). In 1855 Cousins's interpretive talents were fully recognized and reproductive engraving acknowledged as an art form. In this year Cousins became the first English engraver admitted to the full honors of the Royal Academy. Ironically, by the middle of the century, the profession of reproductive engraving was within a generation of obsolescence, soon to be rendered superfluous by photography.

Although the art and profession of translating a painting into ink on paper may be lost, the artifacts remain for our enjoyment. This sequence of prints selected from Amherst's collection illustrates the richness and variety to be found in reproductive print media: richness of technique, images and application.

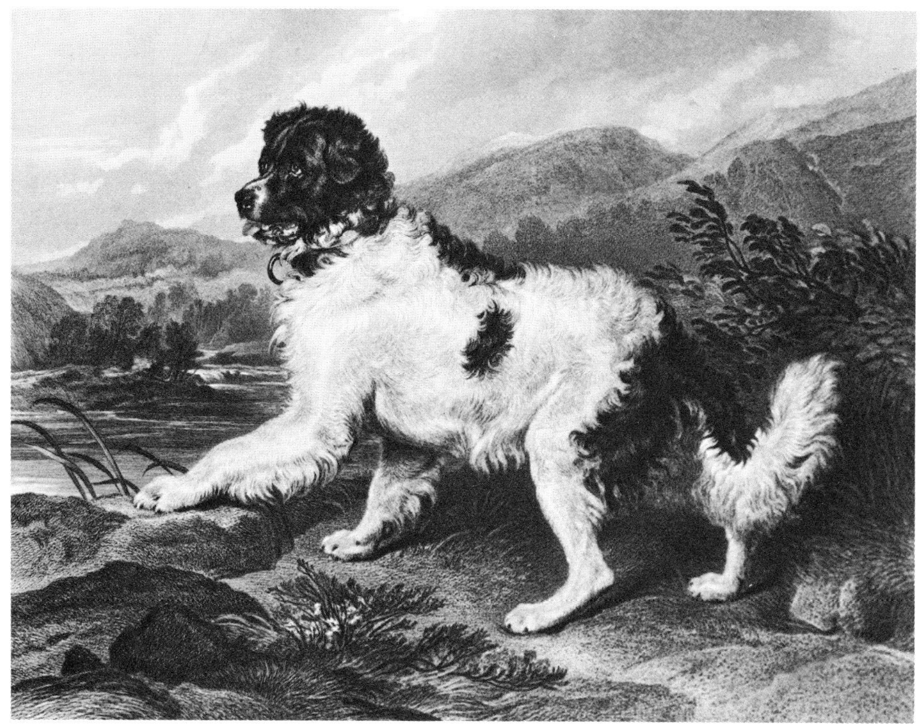

Fig. 8 Charles George Lewis (1808–1880)
 Lion, 1856
 Engraving, 13½ × 17″, after Sir Edwin Henry
 Landseer (1802–1873)
 Museum Purchase
 Pr xx 90

1. See, David Alexander and Richard T. Godfrey, *Painters and Engraving: The Reproductive Print from Hogarth to Wilkie* (New Haven: Yale Center for British Art, 1980); and Brenda D. Rix, *Pictures for the Parlour: The English Reproductive Print from 1775 to 1900* (Toronto: Art Gallery of Ontario, 1983).

2. For a complete catalogue and discussion of Hogarth's prints see, Ronald Paulson, *Hogarth's Graphic Works: First Complete Edition*, 2v. (New Haven: Yale University Press, 1965; revised 1970).

3. Paulson, v. 1, 150–2.

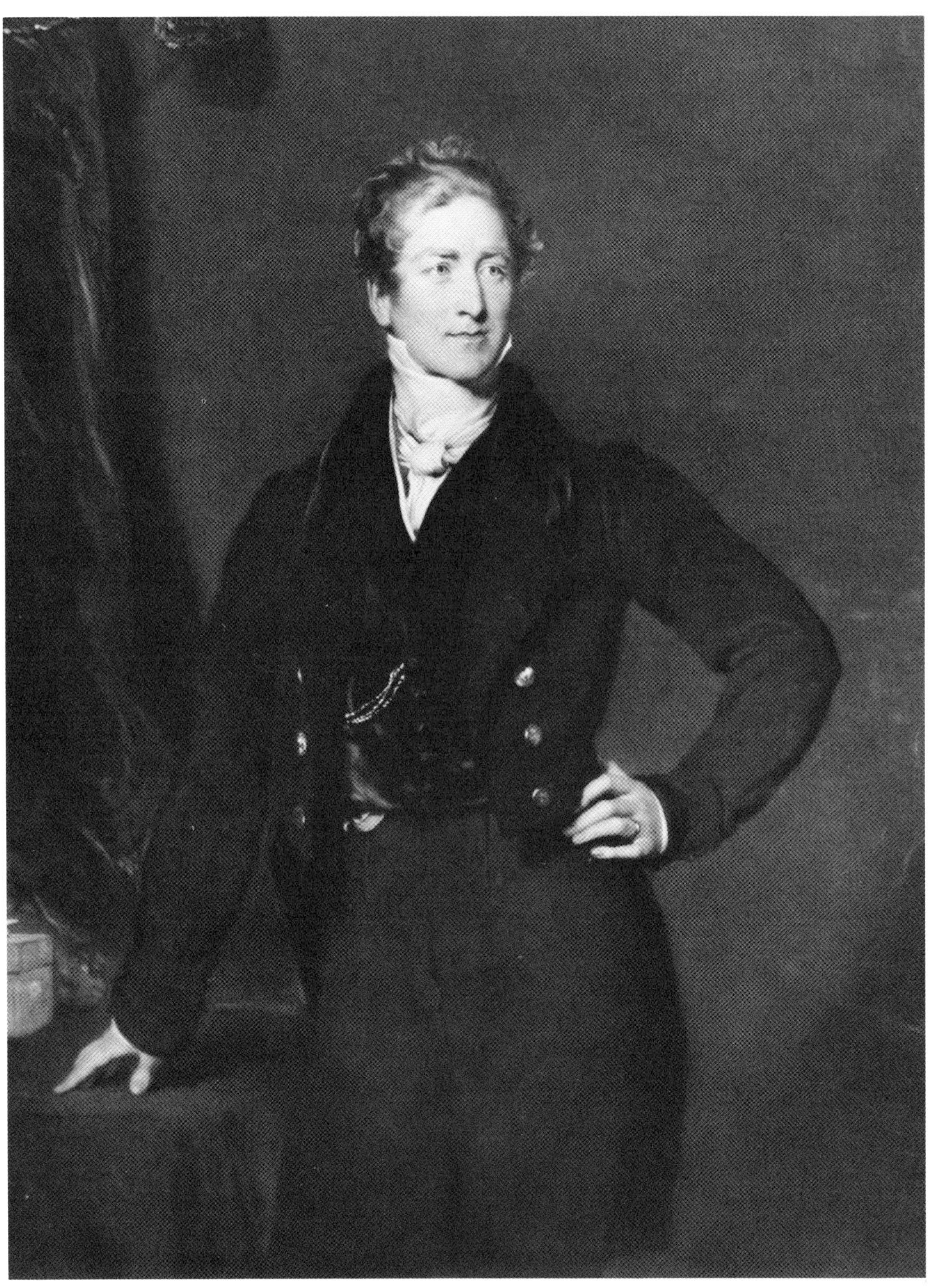

Fig. 9 Samuel Cousins (1804–1887)
Portrait of Sir Robert Peel
Mezzotint engraving, 21½ × 15¾″, after
Sir Thomas Lawrence (1769–1830)
Gift of the Children of Dwight W., '95 and
Elizabeth Morrow
1955.486

4. Paulson, v. 1, 267–75. See also, Georg Christoph Lichtenberg, *Hogarth on High Life: The "Marriage a la Mode,"* trans. and ed. by Arthur S. Wensinger with W.B. Coley (Middletown, Connecticut: Wesleyan University Press, 1970).

5. Alexander and Godfrey, 25. See also, David Alexander, "The Dublin Group: Irish Mezzotint Engravers in London 1750–1775," *Quarterly Bulletin of the Irish Georgian Society,* XVI, 1973, 72–93.

6. Benedict Nicolson, *Joseph Wright of Derby, Painter of Light* (London: Paul Mellon Foundation for British Art, 1968).

7. Andrew Wilton, *Constable's "English Landscape Scenery"* (London: British Museum Publications, 1979).

8. Michael Twyman, *Lithography 1800–1850. The Techniques of Drawing on Stone in England and France and their Application in Works of Topography* (London: Oxford University Press, 1970).

9. Anthony Dyson, "Images Interpreted: Landseer and the Engraving Trade," *Print Quarterly,* v. I, no. 1 (1984), 31–43.

William Blake's *BOOK OF JOB*
by William W. Heath

During the last three years of his life, William Blake (1757–1827) executed what is frequently cited as his greatest achievement as a visual artist: the twenty-two plates comprising the *Illustrations of the Book of Job*. The sum of £150 that John Linnell advanced in 1826 for an edition of 300 sets (proofs sold at 6 guineas, others at three) eased, but did not remove, the poverty in which Blake and his wife Catherine lived, in the one room home-and-studio in Fountain Court, the Strand. It was decades before the Linnell estate recouped the original investment: 68 sets remained unsold at the time of the public sale of the Linnell collection in 1918 (though additional sets may have been printed after the initial 300).[1]

Although Linnell's subsidy was given in response to the series of watercolors about Job that Blake painted for Thomas Butts sometime between 1810 and 1820, Blake's interest in the figure of Job goes back for at least three decades: as a mythic hero who falls and is redeemed, Job's parallel to Blake's Albion (in *Jerusalem*) and Milton (of *The Book of Milton*) is obvious. But this medium for Blake was both new and old: the *Illustrations* is done by copperplate engraving rather than the "illuminated printing" in relief, and the language of the book is not his own but that of the Old and New Testaments. Yet Blake's *Job* is not a series of illustrations for a set Biblical text: it is a radical re-reading (and re-seeing) of that story in an independent art form that will re-present the Hebrew poet's vision in the light of the modern poet's sense of myth and history, uniting for Blake, as Northrop Frye has said, "the work of the creator with that of the teacher."

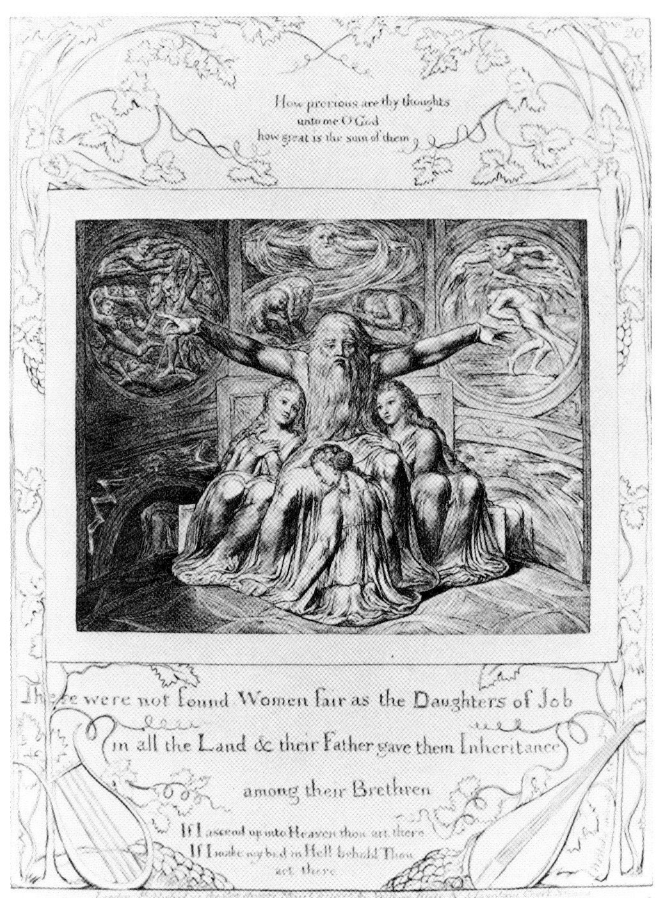

Fig. 1 William Blake, 1757–1827
Illustrations of the Book of Job, 1825
Engraving, "Canst Thou Bind the Sweet Influences of . . ." one of 22 engravings in one bound volume, p. 14
8⅝ × 6⅝"
Gift of Dr. and Mrs. K. Frank Austen '50
1983.44

Fig. 2 William Blake, 1757–1827
Illustrations of the Book of Job, 1825
Engraving, "How Precious are they Thoughts Unto me O God . . ." one of 22 engravings in one bound volume, p. 20
8⅝ × 6⅝"
Gift of Dr. and Mrs. K. Frank Austen '50
1983.44

Some of the modes of Blake's imaginative re-vision of the Biblical text, and his implicit re-ordering of his reader's expectations, can be seen in the accompanying illustrations. In plate XIV (fig. 1), only the horizontal lines of prose at the bottom and top of the plate appear in the Book of Job (in that order): the words in the margins are, of course, slightly altered versions of the story of the creation as it appears in Genesis. In trying to follow this text, the reader's eye crosses the top and bottom of the plate, but then must move down the margins in pursuit of the Genesis words, actually entering several of the pictographs. And the visual design at the center of the plate also requires some iconographic reading: the central figure is obviously God, with his arms extended in the traditional gesture of creation (and crucifixion). Beneath those arms, in opposite directions, move the sun and moon, represented by an Apollo-like figure with horses and a Diana with serpents. But the cloud on which God sits also becomes the roof of a cave enclosing Job (with his wife and the friends), who appears as a sort of mirror image of his creator: their faces, their postures, echoing but not repeating one another. Thus, two-thirds of the way through his version of Job, Blake reminds the reader of the central meaning of the story as he retells it: the story of Job is, for Blake, a myth of the inner life, an account of the way man creates God in his own image, with his own imagination.

In plate XX (fig. 2), the next to last in the volume, the iconography (like the amalgamation of the Psalms with Job in the verbal text) reminds the reader of the essential role of art (including music and song) in any act of human or eternal creation (or redemption): large musical instruments decorate the bottom corners of the plate, while at the design's center Job narrates for his three daughters (parallel perhaps to Milton's) the story of his life, as his outstretched hands (echoing the gesture of God in plate XIV) point to a series of three panels (very Blakean paintings indeed, unlike the cartoon-like pictures in the margins of XIV) that illustrate crucial moments in his own biography (and echo previous plates of this work). Thus Blake, at the end of his own days, creates a work that comments on, reviews (and deconstructs) his own life as a visionary artist and radical religious thinker, whose vocation had consistently been to teach his audience to see, and read, anew.

1. *Editor's Note.* The early editions have been elsewhere described as follows:

> Proof first issue (with proof mark lower right): 65 impressions on French white wove paper plus 150 impressions on chine appliqué (laid india). Published 1825.
> Regular first issue: 100 impressions on French or Whatman paper, without the proof mark. Issued 1826.
> Publication line unchanged apart from 'proof'.
> Linnell edition: 100 sets of chine appliqué (laid india). Publication line unchanged but do not have the proof mark lower right and therefore cannot be confused with first issue, as above. Published 1874. Plates now in the British Museum— presented 1919 by Linnell's descendants.

See, London, William Weston Gallery, Catalogue No. 11, 1985: *The English Vision*, item 3, Note.

The volume at hand has a provenance worthy of comment in its own right. On April 22, 1831 it was presented by the well known English novelist Amelia Opie (1759–1853) to the noted French medalist and sculptor David d'Angers (1789–1856). This was a doubly artistic association, since her husband John Opie (1761–1807) held a wide reputation and, like his wife, enjoyed many associations in literary circles. Amelia Opie's inscription reads: "This work remarkable both for *Genius & Extravagance* is the gift of Amelia Opie to her friend David, whose own genius will make him prize the former while his excellent taste makes it impossible for him to imitate the latter." One of the book plates affixed to that page shows that the book passed on to the possession of another sculptor, Henri-Joseph de Triqueti (1802/4–1874) and thence, into the library of the painter Sir Edward J. Poynter (1836–1919), who had once studied art in Paris. A date of 1886 on Poynter's bookplate would seem to indicate that he acquired the publication after his election to the Royal Academy in 1877, but before his election to the Presidency of that august body in 1896, a post he held until the year before his death. A further inscription indicates that the volume was subsequently purchased (in 1957) from the E. Weyhe Gallery in New York City. Dr. and Mrs. K. Frank Austen '50 presented it to the College in 1983.

VICTORIAN DOMESTICITY
by Frank Trapp

Long the victims of modern critical disrepute, the favorite painters of the Victorian age have once again come to be accepted—if perhaps still without the heady enthusiasm of that former age. Given the vast productivity—almost the redundancy—of painterly output during that era of British ascendance as a commercial and Imperial dominion, the holdings of the Mead Art Museum are indeed modest in number and scope. Still, they do afford more than a glimpse of the larger picture, with its special savours that are so indelibly detectable in the art of other Western nations of the time—not least of all, contemporaneous preferences in the United States. It is now widely agreed, of course, that especially in the early years of Victoria's reign, the natively Germanic tastes of her beloved consort, Prince Albert, affected prevailing standards in his adopted land. But they found so highly compatible a climate there that if anything, they seem not at all alien, but rather, a wholly natural outgrowth of indigenous factors. Most notable among them perhaps was a virtually absolute entrenchment of bourgeois standards in a land where the new economic and political institutions of modern industrialist society had first taken classic shape. Among other traits fostered by those cultural conditions was a delight in dissimulation which rivalled, but in no way imitated, the mock heroics of earlier, Rococo invention. Hence, in an age of unapologetic involvement in exploitation, artistic refuge could be found in carefully nurtured moral conceits which centered above all on the image of innocence and domesticity.

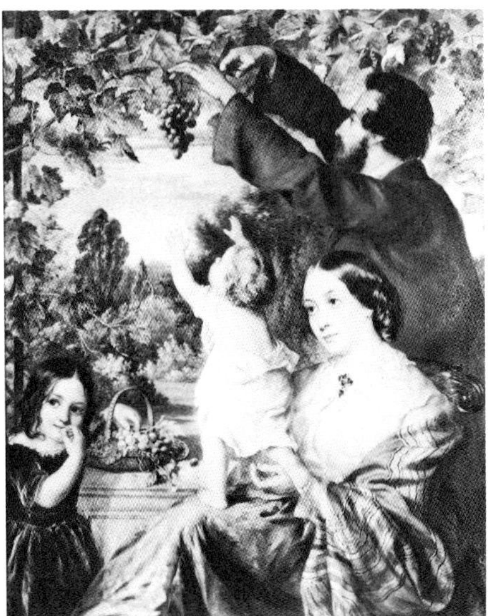

Fig. 1 Sir George Hayter (1792–1871)
Family Portrait With Two Children, 1857
Oil on canvas, 24 × 20″
Museum Purchase
1975.73

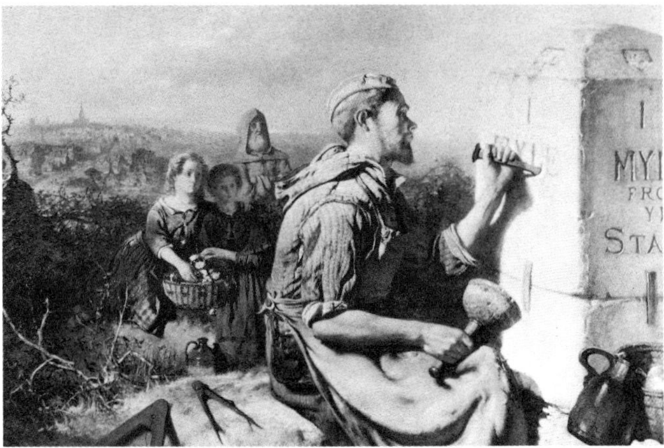

Fig. 2 John Ritchie (Fl. 1858–1875)
The Stone Mason
Oil on canvas, 20 × 30″
Museum Purchase
1979.72

Surely this is the message of a *Family Portrait With Two Children* (fig. 1), painted by Sir George Hayter (1792–1871), a favorite of the Queen, whom he portrayed with conviction and warmth. Hayter here turns to subjects of far lesser social rank whom he elevates to a quasi-religious status, for his is essentially a paraphrase of the traditional Holy Family. One could hardly imagine a more patent compression of the virtues of domesticity than are encapsulated in this sympathetic depiction of Hayter's now unknown bourgeois sitters. He thus extends the traditions of Reynolds (as in his famous *The Age of Innocence*), wherein a specific subject is graced with a larger, symbolic frame of reference. Needless to say, the darker side of the moral universe was also cast in contemporary terms by other Victorian artists, in extension of Hogarth's moralizing genre in which the earliest wholly native British expression took form. So far there is no image of fallen virture or other solemn messages of the time in the repertory of the Mead collection. Perhaps there need not be. At least this sample of the more optimistic side of the Victorian coin suffices to recall the skilled hand and practiced eye of its maker. And in its crisp forms and blond tonalities, with their heightened local colorations, an attractive aspect of the High Victorian mode is nicely summarized.

Closely related in sentiment and manner is a genre painting by a little known yet very capable artist, John Ritchie (fl. 1858–1875), whose *Stone Mason* (fig. 2) celebrates the dignity of work. Again, a religious note is struck in the inclusion of the two young onlookers, with their hint of the future, and of a monkish companion, who seems to speak of tradition and the past. Apparently the scene is set near Stamford in Lincolnshire looking down from the hill toward London.[1] But for all the specific suggestion of the locale and more especially, in the plainspoken visage of the workman, the narrative message is thinly veiled in its symbolic portent. In a far less monumental way, Ritchie's roadside worker is an English counterpart to the images of Courbet or Millet, in which the dignity of labor and sometimes, its human costs, are personified.

Overtones of social awareness implicit in Ritchie's canvas were not uncommon, of course, in the repertory of Victorian artists, and the poignancy of modern human existence was often a theme, as in such masterpieces of the day as Ford Maddox Brown's famous commentary, *The Last of England*. While the Mead collection does not yet include any paintings by Brown or his major Pre-Raphaelite colleagues—leave aside a few drawings by their number—it does contain a fine example of the theatrical and literary preoccupations of the other wing of that company, an *Ophelia* (fig. 3) by Sir Thomas Francis Dicksee (1819–1895). Unlike Sir John Everett Millais' more famous interpretation of Shakespeare's pathetic personage, who is shown in death, floating in the water, Dicksee's Ophelia appears in the last, fated moments of her brief, unhappy life. Pale and drawn of facial feature

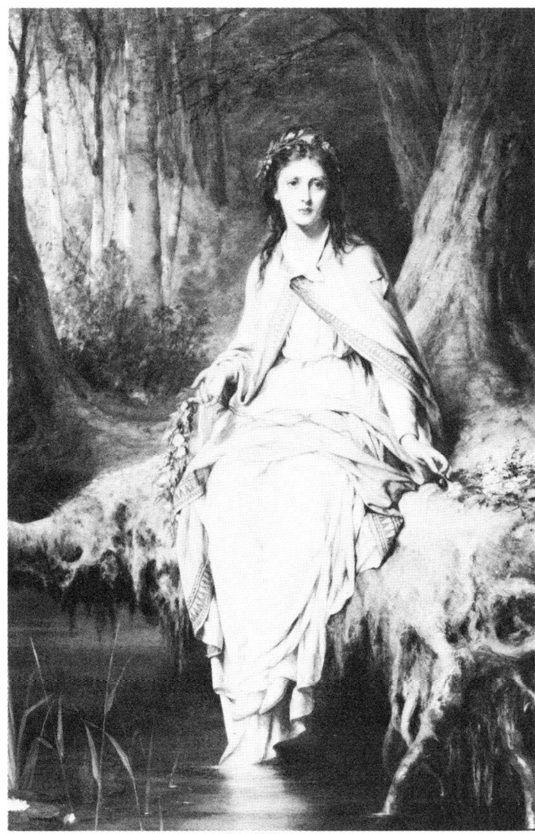

Fig. 3 Thomas Francis Dicksee (1819–1895)
    Ophelia, 1875
    Oil on canvas, 37½ × 24¾"
    Museum Purchase
    1961.4

and dressed in bridal white with a fillet of flowers about her hair, she sits dejectedly on a woodland bank at the side of the stream in which she would find her mortal end. The flowers she holds or that lie nearby, in their own fragility and fleeting beauty, serve only to stress, not relieve, the sense of Ophelia's fatal plight. She is thus isolated as the pathetic victim of the plot, not incorporated as a tragic heroine, as for example, Queen Catherine of Aaragon appears in C. R. Leslie's earlier staging of another Shakespearean theme. As Judith Barter has pointed out in Volume 3 of the Mead Monographs, Leslie's interpretation stands for the more formal, historically oriented staging sought in the first half of the nineteenth-century British School:[2] Dicksee's isolation of the personal and individual, marks a special (may one say, a more intimate) focus, one which belongs to the High Victorian ethos, where the boundaries between sentiment and sentimentality are often put in jeopardy.

As it has been mentioned elsewhere in the present volume, in the discussion of British portraiture, a domestic tone came to be favored widely in the cultural climate of Victorian Britain. To be sure, the inclusion of direct likenesses in representations of historical moments had become an established mode, one that had been widely adopted throughout Europe, as a memorable repertory of historical machines eloquently testifies. The tradition of the "conversation piece" which had been nurtured in Britain remained a healthy enterprise in the capable hands of professional practitioners. The borderlines between strictly portrait representation and the depiction of familiar, anecdotal situations was therefore apt to be indistinct. Such is the case with portraits of the Royal Family by favored artists, including Sir George Hayter. Another of the cadre who served in that capacity was the prolific painter James Sant (1820–1916), who enjoyed the station of Portrait Painter of Queen Victoria, an honor bestowed in 1872. He showed his mettle early in a large group portrait, *The 7th Earl of Cardigan Relating the Story of the Cavalry Charge of Balaclava to the Prince Consort and the Royal Children at Windsor* (1854). The freer, more painterly manner of his mature years is to be admired in such well-known canvases as *Miss Martineau's Garden* (1873), now in the Tate Gallery, and *The Schoolmaster's Daughter*. The latter canvas was presented as Sant's diploma painting following his election as a full member of the Royal Academy in 1869. It was shown at the Academy in 1871 and remains in the collection of that institution.

A smaller, wholly informal portrayal by Sant of an attractive but unknown sitter was recently purchased for the Amherst College collection. Titled, *Light Thrown on a Dark Passage* (fig. 4), it is an especially appealing example of the melding of the portrait and genre traditions in its period. At the same time, it beautifully exemplifies the sensitivity to individual, personal identity that was cultivated by artists of Sant's class and the technical prowess they could regularly summon to their tasks. It is thus a fitting complement to the other Victorian works in the Collection, as well as to echoes of the

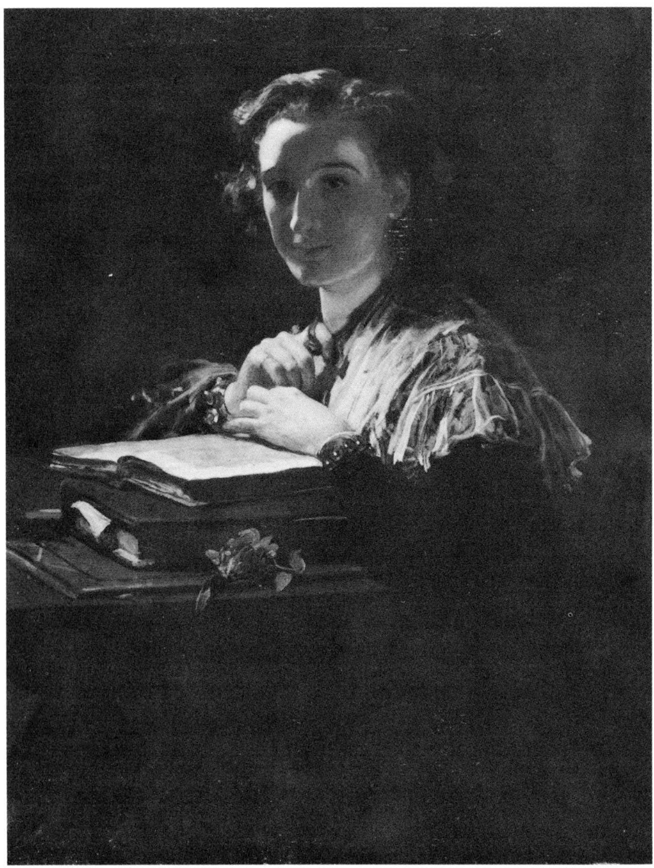

Fig. 4 James Sant (1820–1916)
Light Thrown on a Dark Passage
Oil on canvas, 36 × 30″
Museum Purchase
1985.31

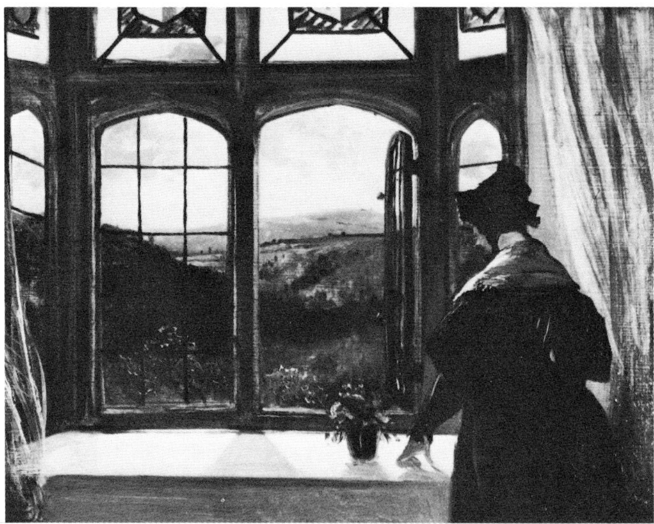

Fig. 5 Sir Edwin Henry Landseer (1802–1873)
The Duchess of Bedford, 1829–30
Oil on canvas, 10⅛ × 12⅛″
Museum Purchase
1978.112

same tastes for reticent but strong feminine presences in the *oeuvre* of such American counterparts as Eastman Johnson (1824–1906), in his beautiful portrait of Edwina Booth (1885), also in the Mead collection.

Even less a "portrait" in the usual sense of the word is a charming oil sketch of an interior with the *Duchess of Bedford* (fig. 5) painted by Sir Edwin Landseer (1802–1873). Reputedly a replica of a larger version of the subject which was owned by the Duke of Bedford (present whereabouts unknown), Landseer's precious little scene is appropriately possessed of qualities of visual scale which vastly exceed the actual physical size of the picture. Son of a well-known engraver, John Landseer, the aspiring young artist was trained at the Royal Academy and at an early age, in 1831, was honored with the status of full membership in the Academy. While Landseer's huge reputation amongst his contemporaries was based upon his virtuosity as an animalier—famed in particular for his spirited images of dogs, stags, and lions—he was gifted as a portraitist of humans, as well.

Reportedly, Landseer and the 2nd Duchess of Bedford (1781–1853) enjoyed a long and intimate relationship, despite the fact that the noblewoman was his senior by some 20 years. His several other representations of the lady portray her in characteristically active roles—on horseback, at a reception, or fashionably dressed for a ball. Since this particular depiction shows her in a subdued situation and attired in a matronly black, it may date from the time of the death of her husband, in 1839, and not as it may otherwise be inferred, from an earlier period, when Landseer was a frequent visitor to the Bedford household at Endsleigh, near Milton Abbey in Devon. However, an old inscription on the back of the academy board on which the picture is painted situates the setting as at Woburn Abbey.[3] Whatever the case, the architectural setting is convincing and evocative of the early Gothic Revival—or perhaps of the *survival* of medieval forms in Renaissance structures, as may be seen in the "Rotherwas Room," now installed as an interior ensemble in the Mead Art Museum.[4] Questions of the actual locale aside, there can be no doubt of the painter's fluency of touch or of the conviction with which he summarizes a wealth of visual information, as he shows the Duchess gazing from her elevated station point upon the spreading landscape that surrounds the family seat.

Despite today's penchant for recurrent reappraisal of our predecessors and the widespread enthusiasm for Victorian artifacts—with all their ebullience and overstatement—not all viewers may be won over by artistic efforts of the foregoing character. They nevertheless represent a significant episode in our heritage, one hardly restricted to the British scene alone. As with the "new academicism" which has recently claimed a freshly respectable place in the contemporary creative development, one is alerted by the exemplars of Victorian art of the vulnerability of fashion and at the same time, of its powers of survival and renewal, as well. *Sic transit gloria artis mundi.*

1. See, Mead Museum documentary files.

2. See, *Mead Monograph Vol. V: Nineteenth-Century American Art,* Judith A. Barter, "Frank Millet and Nineteenth-Century American Painting," p. 8. It might be further noted in this context that the Collection also contains a small study by Daniel Maclise (1811–1870): *Claudio and Isabella,* oil on panel, 8 × 11″, Gift of Prof. Arthur H. Baxter, June, 1937. The vogue for Shakespearean subjects had come into particular favor during the late eighteenth century, under the sponsorship above all of the entrepreneur John Boydell (1719–1804), whose celebrated "Shakespeare Gallery" was situated on Pall Mall. In 1802 it housed some 102 canvases by famous artists (including Reynolds, Kauffmann, Opie and others) which appeared that year in a large volume of reproductive engravings. Leslie brought to that tradition his personal flair for the theatrical.

3. The documentary report on the picture and the bibliographical information compiled for the Roy Miles Gallery, from whom the work was purchased for the Mead Museum, provides further details on the relationship of the painter and the Duchess. See, Mead Museum documentary files.

4. See, *Mead Monograph Vol. III: Decorative Arts at Amherst College,* Winter 1981–82.